12-2-74

TWO TO GET READY

two
to get
ready

ANTHONY FLORIO, Ph.D.

FLEMING H. REVELL COMPANY
OLD TAPPAN, NEW JERSEY

Library of Congress Cataloging in Publication Data

Florio, Anthony.
    Two to get ready.

    1. Marriage. I. Title.
BV835.F55   248'.4   74-10549
ISBN 0-8007-0676-5

MY THANKS TO

Marj for challenging me to write a book directed to engaged couples.

Evelyn for making this book a reality. You are a joy and an inspiration.

Dawn, Leslie, and *Joan,* the daughters who reflect my pride and love.

Joan, a wonderful example of what God intended a mate to be . . . I love you!

Contents

Why Prepare for Marriage?

Most of you reading this book today will be married within the next five years. When you *do* marry you and your partner will be entering the most significant human relationship of your lives. Yet many of you will spend less time preparing for this new life-style than you will spend on learning to drive a car, to ride the surf, to speak a foreign language. As a result, your marriage may be a disappointment. Preparing for a good marriage takes time, study, and discipline. Are you willing to make this investment in your future?

In the United States at the present time, one of three marriages ends in divorce. And among many other thousands of couples an emotional divorce exists, although the marriage is still legally intact. This trend has a significant impact on the church. The divorce rate among Christians is alarming. It is possible for you to become a divorce statistic.

Having Jesus Christ in your life doesn't automatically guarantee success in your marriage. As Christians you have the same basic needs that all people have, including the need to love and be loved, and to give sexual expression to that love. God Himself created a mate for Adam, and so sanctified the marriage relationship. But if your needs and those of your mate are not met in marriage, where should the blame be placed?

In my profession as a premarriage, marriage, and family counselor I have seen hundreds of couples whose disturbed marriages were the result of inadequate preparation for marriage. They didn't know themselves well, they didn't understand their motivations for negative behavior, they knew even less about their mates before marriage — and they didn't realize the dozens of hang-ups that they both had developed from childhood experiences and relationships.

Many times I have thought how much better it would have been for them to have had professional counseling *before* they married. Prevention would have been so much better than patching up a disintegrating relationship. And so my purpose in writing this book is a fourfold one:

1. To prevent some problems in marriage by helping you to evaluate and understand yourself and your problem potential.
2. To encourage you to start to work on your potential problem areas *before* marriage.
3. To focus your attention on the chief cause of problems inside and outside of marriage — the violation of biblical principles of effective living and interpersonal relationships.
4. To encourage you to adopt these biblical principles as a way of life — fulfilling the purpose of God that Christians are to be conformed to the image of His Son.

I don't know the answers to *all* of your questions, or the solutions to *all* of your problems. So reading this book won't guarantee you a happy marriage. But hopefully it will be helpful — and may prevent you from becoming a divorce statistic.

Part 1

MAKING THE MOST OF YOURSELF

1

Are You Ready for Marriage?

THE CASE FOR MARRIAGE

What is marriage? Marriage is all sorts of things to all kinds of people and to define it successfully is difficult. But a reasonably good definition might be:

> Marriage is a unique relationship between a man and a woman through which both seek to give and to receive satisfaction of their needs.

Had Adam and Eve not sinned we probably would not have had any unfulfilled needs. We would have a healthy identity enjoying problem-free relationships in an unspoiled, uncontaminated environment. By the time a person reaches his late teens he can reasonably evaluate his life and form at least a tentative philosophy. And he can accept the fact that he is, like all human beings, imperfect and therefore defective physically, mentally, emotionally, and spiritually. The child

15

born today is faced with the cumulative effects of man's sinful disobedience since the beginning of the human race.

God knows the makeup of these defective humans whom He loves, and so He created the family unit in which man's basic needs could be met satisfactorily:

1. The *physical* needs for oxygen, nourishment, exercise, sexual expression, and sleep.
2. The *mental* needs for purposeful thought and creative work.
3. The *emotional* need to love and be loved; to be accepted.
4. The *spiritual* need for fellowship with God.

Children growing up now and in the future will find it more difficult than previous generations to have their needs met satisfactorily. The traveling nuclear-age family develops a sense of rootlessness. Children of these families have the emotional need for love and acceptance which generates confidence. But these needs are difficult to satisfy within the framework of a family life-style where one or both parents are away from home for extended periods because of the demands of their careers, or even on a daily basis where the family circle is not complete until late in the evening. Perhaps economic necessity forces the mother to work or the father to hold two jobs. The present-day family unit does not usually include the grandparents, aunts, uncles, and cousins that often were included in the living arrangements of the extended family of two generations ago. So there are no other family members to take up the pressures generated by absent parents. This has been, in part, responsible for the search to create other family life-styles, like communal living, providing for a father figure in the house most of the time.

In my study of families where polygamous relationships exist, I find that disillusionment usually sets in because conflicts arise due to jealousy among the wives, favoritism among the children, and eventually a feeling of insecurity among many of the participants. I endorse the traditional monogamous life-style, and in this book we will be focusing on preparing for that kind of marriage relationship.

Therefore shall a man leave his father and his mother, and shall cleave unto his wife: and they shall be one flesh.

Genesis 2:24

GOAL: HAPPINESS

In different cultures there are different measures for the success of a marriage. They include: the husband's ability to support his family and accumulate material wealth; the husband's ability to father a large family; the couple's ability to rear the children in the accepted mores and social patterns of the society; the wife's skill as a homemaker; or the fact that the couple remains in the marriage relationship for a lifetime.

However, the American ideal is a marriage in which

personal happiness has become a valid goal. No matter how well the marriage may fulfill society's expectations, unless the couple is genuinely happy, the marriage is not considered a success.

How does one define happiness? It would seem easier to indicate the factors in marriage that must be present, at least for most couples, in order for them to feel that the relationship is a happy one.

1. A strong emotional bond of affection and mutual caring about each other's needs, including the willingness to sacrifice for the other's benefit.
2. Enjoyment of each other's personality as a companion, implying many shared interests and mutual goals.
3. Respect for each other as individuals.
4. A sexual attraction for each other and a mutually satisfactory pattern of expressing love and commitment through sexual intercourse.
5. A sense of permanence in the marriage.
6. For Christians, a shared conviction of the relationship of marriage as having been instituted by God and therefore having the added dimension of spiritual values.

HAZARD AHEAD: TEEN MARRIAGE

I find many young couples coming for premarriage counseling who feel that achieving happiness in marriage is a very "iffy" thing and unpredictable. They believe that if difficulties arise that require some time and effort to resolve, either before or after marriage, then they obviously were not meant for each other and should break up, or if married, get a divorce, so that each will be free for another try. Such an attitude is symptomatic of an unwillingness to assume responsibility and an inability to cope with problem-solving. These two negative traits are indications that these couples are not mature enough to marry yet and achieve a happy, lasting relationship.

Premarriage counseling exists to uncover potential problem areas in individual personalities and in areas of interaction between the future spouses. A counselor can help you become objective enough to assess *beforehand* the probability of achieving happiness in your marriage.

Some of the couples who come for counseling and who feel that "if marriage doesn't work out we'll just call it quits" are still in high school. The pat answer to their problem might seem to be that they're too young for marriage. But other couples with the same attitude are in their mid-twenties, and this wouldn't be considered too young by today's standards. When a counselor advises against high-school marriages he doesn't base that advice solely on the fact that the couples are very young. He is also aware that statistics show that when both marriage partners are under twenty-one, the failure rate of their marriages is six times higher than marriages between couples ten years older. One half of all the divorces granted in the United States involve couples under twenty years old, whereas

only one marriage in ten involving the over-twenty-
five couple ends in divorce. And couples who marry
after completing their college education have a better-
than-average chance of staying married.

ARE YOU MATURE ENOUGH?

The implication here is that maturity usually, but
not always, increases with age and experience. The
more mature a person is the more successful his marriage is likely to be. Just what do we mean by mature?
The dictionary definition doesn't quite fit our context
in this discussion: "fully developed," "ripe" are given
as synonyms. But maturity in the sense that we are
thinking of is a relative thing. We may be mature
enough at age six to enter school and attend to some of
our needs like eating, dressing, etc., but we are not mature enough at that age to understand the high-school
curriculum or to exercise complete control over all of
our needs. Maturing is a process involving growth and,
except in the physical sense, few if any of us ever
achieve complete maturity on all levels of our personality.

But we do recognize that marriage requires a level
of maturity that includes willingness to assume responsibility for our own actions, for our own welfare,
plus the welfare of a mate and children. It includes
vocational readiness, the ability to earn a living that
will provide adequately for one's family. In some circumstances the parents of college-student married
couples agree to pay their expenses until graduation.

This situation requires a level of maturity that will enable both young people to strike a fine balance in their attitudes towards their helping parents. They need an appropriate appreciation for the valuable contribution their parents are making and a constant awareness that such help doesn't bind them to the dictates of their parents. Unfortunately, many parents do not give help without invisible strings attached — conditions that may threaten a cutoff of funds if the young couple does not comply. Such family situations can cause deep resentments in grown children and their parents, and add deep and divisive emotional burdens to a young marriage.

If you are having such problems you might find the Public Affairs Pamphlet Number 355, *Young Adults and Their Parents,* helpful (for information write Public Affairs Pamphlets, 381 Park Avenue South, New York, New York 10016).

A young person contemplating marriage ought to be mature enough to recognize his or her reasons for wanting to marry and to judge correctly whether those reasons are adequate. A girl who rushes into marriage to escape an unhappy homelife isn't acting responsibly. After marrying, the probability is that there will be two unhappy individuals. Or the couple who do not love each other, who have nothing in common, whose dispositions clash, who come from totally different backgrounds frequently marry when the girl finds she is pregnant. They marry "for the sake of the child" and condemn that child to emotional crippling. This is immature reasoning and irresponsible behavior.

Becoming mature enough to marry ought also to include learning the motivations for your actions and how to control your behavior. The person who lives at the mercy of his instincts is a menace to himself and others.

A very young couple have not lived long enough to experience many of the situations that alone can teach them mature responses. The learning process is, to some extent, a trial-and-error proposition. We are confronted with situations for which at times there are no correct or incorrect answers. Sometimes we respond wisely, at other times not so wisely, but we begin to amass a data bank of information based on the consequences of the actions we took. Reason alone would indicate that the more practice you acquire in decision-making, through situations confronted, the greater will be the resources for capable decision-making when the need arises. So when parents, or pastors, or professional counselors advise against early marriage or teen marriage, the reason may not be merely because you are too young, but that you are not yet mature enough to handle all that is implied in the marriage relationship.

MARRIAGE MEANS RESPONSIBILITY

What do we mean by this phrase, "all that is implied in the marriage relationship"? In spite of the impression given by advertisers, TV, movies, and popular fiction, you won't spend most of your married life in bed or sitting on a couch holding hands. The greater part of your life together won't be spent surfing, either, or walking hand in hand through a field of flowers. Your wife won't look great in a bathing suit forever. Your husband may go without a shave or leave his dirty socks on the floor. And there may be times when you'd like to give your children back.

Children? But you may be planning to marry in your teens, grow up together (there's no satisfactory way of doing this without putting enormous strain on the marriage), and avoid having a family until you've outgrown your immaturity and are ready for parenthood—a plan I hear frequently when I am asked to counsel with teen-age couples. In spite of the Pill and the best intentions, brides *do* get pregnant, and successful parenthood requires more than the ability to procreate, to prepare a formula, and to change diapers.

When you bring into the world another human being, you have given life to more than a physical organism, you have created an individual who will become the sum total of his genetic inheritance, plus his interpersonal relationships and his own will. But beyond this, he will also be a living soul, one who will have the opportunity to accept eternal life through his relationship with Jesus Christ, or who will forfeit that experience and be separated eternally from God, through his unwillingness to believe. The sexual relationship of a man and woman carries with it the possibility, if not the probability, of this kind of responsibility. If you aren't mature enough to assume the role of a parent, then you are not mature enough for marriage.

GROWING UP?

But let's get back to that idea of marrying very young and "growing up together." In my profession, I am dedicated first to the idea of prevention, then to the concept of resolving problems — or at least improving the marital relationship. The immature person, whatever his age, has many problems, and the last thing he needs is to marry and acquire *more* problems. Making a success of your marriage is a full-time job that will require physical stamina, mental acuity, objective reasoning, emotional stability, love and consideration, and the spiritual insight and power that comes from the Holy Spirit living in you and directing your life.

There are inevitable strains put upon a marriage by just learning to adapt to each other in a completely new life-style. If, in addition to this, both of you are trying to work on your own inadequacies, negative traits, and hang-ups so that you can become mature, or "grow up together," the stage is set for a shaky marriage, and the possibility that you will "blow up" rather than "grow up."

TWO CHILDREN

One case history in my practice illustrates the far-reaching consequences of marrying before one is mature enough to accept the responsibilities of marriage and parenthood. My client is a girl nineteen years old.

She hates her two-year-old son because he represents the reason why she is trapped in a marriage. She got married as soon as she found she was pregnant but she feels she should be in college. She is starving intellectually. Now she is wrestling with pots and pans and diapers when she should be in school wrestling with ideas. Her son reminds her of her husband whom she didn't like even when she married him. When I asked her why she neglected her son, she replied, "How can a child be a mother to another child?"

Fortunately, this young woman wants to learn to love her husband and her son. But many others trapped in similar situations do not have even this much going for them. They feel they have missed too much living. They want to divorce their husbands, put their child or children up for adoption, and go back and relive their adolescent years with all the experiences they have missed.

DO YOU KNOW SOMEONE LIKE THIS?

Sue acts immaturely and cries to get her own way. Troubles overwhelm her and she can't seem to cope. She keeps telling her steady date that she needs him — that she depends on him. He's so big and strong and capable. He is flattered and is about to get engaged to her. But wait a minute! He ought to ask himself first, "Why does she behave in such an immature way?" He thinks it's cute right now, how she dotes on him, and hangs on him, and seems so helpless without him. But if he honestly asks why, and gets professional help to find out, he will find that Sue's mother still has a tremendous influence over her.

Sue has always felt that the way to earn her mother's approval and love was to obey her implicitly. When Sue was little her mother would pick her up and cuddle her and tell her how much "mother loves her good little girl." As a result the girl grew to equate love with obedience. But when she was growing up she resented her loss of freedom, the curtailment of her own wishes and preferences in relation to clothes, amusements, friends, choice of a vocation, and other things in order to conform to what her mother wanted.

TRANSFERRING FEELINGS

She grew up to be an obedient, immature, dependent, resentful human being. If she marries she probably will transfer the resentment she has felt toward her mother to her husband. She felt she could not safely show resentment for all those early years because her mother would stop loving her. But she could feel secure in taking out her resentment on him because his love for her was not bought with the price of obedience.

But can you imagine how bewildered and upset her husband would be because of all the resentment-inspired negative behavior that she might direct toward him? This could include doling out her love-making at specified intervals as a reward for his obeying her wishes in some other area—the same sort of pattern she would have picked up from her mother when she was growing up. And if her husband did not obey she would cry and have a tantrum, sometimes ending with the words her mother had used, "If you really loved me you'd do what I ask."

This young woman is not mature enough for marriage, although she is almost twenty-four, so maturity does *not* automatically come with living a certain number of years. I have seen some young people who were more mature than their parents and grandparents, but I've seen many more who needed help to achieve the kind of maturity that is necessary in order to be a good marriage partner.

LEARNING ABOUT MARRIAGE

Many marriages fail because the partners haven't learned how to be good mates. Often *their* parents didn't know how to be good marriage partners either, and so their kids got fouled up.

If this has been your experience then I'm assuming that you're ready to ask a question like this: "I haven't been taught about marriage as a kid, so now I want to learn. How can I? Teach me." From listening to hundreds of couples, some very young, others in what we would consider the marrying bracket, and still others past those ages, I find that certain repetitive problems plague people. There are often no simple answers, but it is possible for me to give you some hints and helps. I want to cause you to *think,* and then I hope you will be willing to apply what you have learned.

First, if you have admitted that you don't know

what you'd like to know about marriage, you have plenty of company because most people marry without adequate preparation. When such marriages become shaky the partners often blame their parents for not teaching them and preparing them. But they forget that these parents were raised by *their* parents who obviously didn't teach *them*, either.

HELP AVAILABLE

I hope you won't continue along this line of least resistance, hoping for the best — because "after all, what can you do about it?" There is no excuse for a couple planning marriage to drift along in the relationship, wishing for wisdom and not doing anything about it. There is no excuse for our families to be in the mess they are in, even allowing for the problem of evil, because there are books available, especially the Bible, which present the principles of healthy interaction. Some Bible passages point out man's inability to live successful, productive lives without guidance from the God who created them. And the unhappy condition of the world today is living proof.

All we like sheep have gone astray; we have turned every one to his own way; and the Lord hath laid on him the iniquity of us all.

Isaiah 53:6

But the Bible also gives us hope.

> As he looked at the vast crowds he was deeply
> moved with pity for them, for they were as be-
> wildered and miserable as a flock of sheep with no
> shepherd.
>
> Matthew 9:36 PHILLIPS

> My sheep recognise My voice and I know who
> they are. They follow Me and I give them eternal
> life. They will never die and no one can snatch
> them out of My hand.
>
> John 10:27, 28 PHILLIPS

People, like sheep, go astray. Sheep don't know what's best for them, and we don't know what's best for us. Knowing our condition, God has provided an answer to our dilemma—a shepherd—or leader—Jesus Christ who loves us, who is concerned with every detail of our existence and who has provided eternal life for us as a gift. When we invite that Shepherd to come into our lives, because we cannot save ourselves, He accepts that invitation. Then He gives us His Holy Spirit so that we can stop being ignorant sheep and appropriate the mind of Christ. We have the capacity to be ignorant, but also, unlike sheep, we can choose to learn, and God gives us that choice.

We are made in the image of God. We have a mind. We feel emotion. We don't have to be reduced to the existence of sheep. People who lead aimless lives many times produce children who perpetuate this same kind of aimlessness in their own lives, becoming a drain on society.

The Jews are God's chosen people. They have had the reputation of being brilliant businessmen. They know the value of education and pursue it. But God still called these people, these capable people, sheep and offered to become their shepherd. In most homes where the marriage is failing and where the kids are reacting with negative behavior patterns and sometimes antisocial acts, these people are trying to run their lives without a shepherd, too. And in many dating relationships where the couples are looking forward to marriage, the value of choosing Christ as their shepherd has been ignored.

PERSONAL EXPERIENCE

One of the most significant factors in my own life in regard to the way I perform my roles is related to the leadership of Christ in my life.

Many of you have been challenged to make Jesus the Lord of your life as well as your Saviour. This means to let God be the architect of your life. God not only serves as planner, but He also gives power to perform the roles that you are called on to fill. This includes the roles of husband and wife, or parents, and all the other relationships that life entails. God did this for me without destroying my individuality and personality.

At the time of my conversion I was an accordionist and cellist in the band at West Point. I had spent many years learning to play those instruments. Many times I practiced several hours a day and when you have put that much time into something it becomes very dear to you. So music was a very important part of my life.

I had become a Christian, but then I began wondering what God was going to do with my life. I could hardly divorce my interest in music from what God might have in mind for my future. I was sure He would use my musical talent in whatever plans would materialize for a future career. I had surrendered my life completely to God, or so I thought, but I was sure He wouldn't ask me to give up my music. Then one day I realized that although a career without music was unthinkable to me, I had to allow God that option if I really meant business. I remember getting to the point where I said to God, "Lord, I'm willing to even put my music aside if that's what you want me to do." In a sense, I was willing to put a knife through those instruments just as Abraham had been willing to sacrifice Isaac. In my case, God replaced the music profession with a more fulfilling profession.

DEDICATION

I'm wondering if this isn't where some Christians fall down. They have accepted Jesus Christ as their Saviour and in a sense He serves as "fire insurance." But they have never taken that step to allow God to be the architect of their lives. They've never committed their lives completely into God's hands and so they're floundering around trying to do the best they can by their own efforts.

Why is it so important for Christians to be willing

to sacrifice anything and anyone that stands in the way of their putting God first in their lives? Because God calls every Christian to a life of faith. The Bible tells us that without faith it is impossible to please God. We need to learn to exercise our faith in many areas, and one of these is faith in God's willingness and ability to direct our lives to conform to the plan which He has for us. And nothing or no one should be allowed to keep us from being completely free to do God's will.

So it is smart for Christians to realize that left on our own, we will follow the pattern of sheep, endangering our own lives and putting into precarious situations the lives of others. We must realize that we can be as vulnerable as sheep without a shepherd, also.

> Awake! be on the alert! Your enemy the devil, like a roaring lion, prowls round looking for someone to devour.
>
> 1 Peter 5:8 NEB

Those persons who settle for a kind of aimless lifestyle, without meaning and purpose, are most susceptible to being destroyed. Many do find themselves literally destroyed, physically, emotionally, and spiritually. Recognizing the lordship of Christ is the key for giving purpose to your life and for insuring a happy and abundant life together when you marry.

SUPPOSE YOU DON'T MARRY

But suppose you don't marry, what then? Some of you reading this may feel that you are unmarriageable. This seems to be the thinking of young women who have not been popular at school and have the impression that they don't appeal to men. Research has shown that a high percentage of young people who were rated very popular in high school did not do well either academically or socially at the college level. Follow-up studies after they married indicated that on the average their marriages were rated only fair or poor. This was not always the case, obviously, but it occurred often enough to pose the question, "Is popularity in high school a good indication of a person's ability to contract a happy marriage?" And the answer is no. The seeming strength of the popular student, his exercise of many talents and abilities, is often a cover-up for his deficiencies. He feels he must excel in ways that will command attention, in order to constantly reassure himself that he is a worthwhile person.

So don't base your marriageability rating on your high-school-popularity rating. The chances of your marrying will be greatly increased if you are an emotionally healthy person with a good self-image — a person who is able to interact easily with others and who has a genuine interest in other people. It is far more important to *be* the right person than to *find* the right person. So if you can be honest with yourself, acknowledge your deficiencies and try to change them to positive qualities, you will be taking a giant step towards becoming the right partner.

ALTERNATIVES

If you are a Christian you will want to pray about this matter of marriage and ask God to guide you. Because you do not seem to be sought after as a dating partner right now does not necessarily mean that it is God's will for you to remain unmarried. Some Christians seem to feel that all they have to do is sit and wait and God will drop their intended mate on their doorstep. If this is the way you feel, then you are not allowing God the option of providing you with a mate in some other way—perhaps by meeting him or her at a night-school class, in a volunteer activity, a political club, or civic project. You may meet in a college-and-career group if you visit another church, or at a Bible conference where young adults from many states attend. It may be a choral group, a great-books-discussion group, a painting class, a church visitation program. Or it may be while you are collecting donations for the Red Cross, the March of Dimes, or some other project.

Perhaps you like to travel. If you haven't yet formed a strong attachment for some particular area of the country, why not consider trying out entirely different areas of the United States as a home? You'll be exposed to a different life-style, interesting local customs, and varying climates. You'll meet some fascinating people and develop some new friendships. And who can tell what else?

But if you never marry, that isn't a disaster either. There are many single people who live interesting, productive lives and many others who, because they are free from the responsibilities of marriage, live uniquely adventurous lives. Still others feel that God has called them to the single state because of a special ministry and they are able to devote themselves wholeheartedly to their mission in life, without regrets or resentment. Some young people have felt that the time of Christ's Second Coming is so close that they want to spend their years reaching as many people as possible with the gospel. They want to be free to go anywhere an opportunity opens, without feeling that they are neglecting the responsibilities of marriage and parenthood, and so they choose not to marry.

Whatever life-style you opt for, as a Christian you will want to fulfill God's will for you — growing to be more like Jesus Christ.

For those whom He foreknew — of whom He was aware and loved beforehand — He also destined from the beginning (foreordaining them) to be molded into the image of His Son [and share inwardly His likeness], that He might become the first-born among many brethren.

Romans 8:29 AMPLIFIED

QUESTIONS FOR DISCUSSION

1. What factors do you think make marriage a unique relationship?

2. How would you defend legal marriage in light of the trend towards couples merely living together?
3. What do you think is behind the attitude, "If our marriage doesn't work out, we'll just call it quits?"
4. What are the advantages and disadvantages of a couple marrying in their teens?
5. What are the arguments for and against the idea that there is just one person in this world who is right for you?

2

Understanding Yourself

Why is it important to try to gain some self-under-standing? The obvious answer, of course, is that you will become a more knowledgeable person. But there are other reasons, too.

1. If you know your strong points, you can develop them.
2. If you know your weak points, you can correct them.
3. If you do both of these things, you will become a happier person.
4. Happy people are more apt to attract a marriage partner than an unhappy person would.
5. Happy, well-adjusted people tend to have good, stable, fulfilling, permanent marriages.
6. This means that they will affect another person's life positively rather than negatively.
7. This also means that they will become good

parents who will raise happy, well-adjusted
children.

8. These children will most likely grow up without
the emotional crippling that handicaps the children of unhappy, maladjusted parents, and they
will perpetuate good, stable family units when
they marry.

9. God's standard for our lives and His will for us is
that we might be conformed to the image of His
Son. Any steps we take to encourage our development as whole persons will be motivated
by the Holy Spirit and in God's will; therefore,
we can confidently expect God to answer our
prayers for this process.

10. We will become more effective channels for
transmitting God's love, as reflected in the gospel
to others.

IMPERFECT BEGINNINGS

Some of you who are reading this chapter may be
sitting at home, alone. Couples may be reading this
together. Some of you are in a classroom, others may
perhaps be part of an informal discussion group. There
will be many differences among you. Age, sex, education, family background, financial resources, spiritual
level, personality, interests, goals—all of these things
point up your differences. But there is one fact that
unites you with every other human being on this earth
—you are an imperfect person. We all were born with
innate selfish tendencies, and we were brought up by

imperfect parents and the line stretches back through history to our first parents, Adam and Eve.

And to Adam He said: Because you have yielded to your wife's suggestion and have eaten from the tree concerning which I gave you orders, Do not eat of it, cursed is the soil on your account; by toil you shall eat from it all your life . . . . In the sweat of your brow you must make a living until you return to the ground, because out of it you were taken; for dust you are and to dust you shall return.

Genesis 3:17, 19 BERKELEY

For there is no distinction to be made anywhere: everyone has sinned; everyone falls short of the beauty of God's plan.

Romans 3:22, 23 PHILLIPS

IMPROPER PREPARATION

You are aware that you are not performing your roles perfectly as sons and daughters, brothers and sisters, students, citizens, dating partners, and all the other roles you are called on to assume. Perhaps you are still emotionally tied to your parents. You may be unusually shy and very introverted. Or you may be the opposite, emotionally independent of your parents but brash, belligerent, and opinionated. You may be selfish, or too generous—trying to buy others' esteem. You may be repressed to the point of denying your own sexuality, or you may be uninhibited to the point of sexual promiscuity. There are hundreds of problems and as many variations and combinations. But most of the time your parents probably started this problem by not preparing you properly for life's demands.

This is another way of saying that your parents probably violated one or more biblical principles and the results showed up years later as behavioral problems. The Bible is looked on by some individuals as a guidebook for one's spiritual life. But it is far more than that. The precepts put forth in the Word of God, if followed, would enable individuals to be healthier physically, mentally, emotionally, and spiritually. Interaction between individuals, having been motivated and controlled by love, would produce more harmonious relationships.

TRAIN A CHILD

There is a familiar Bible verse that states a principle that, if followed by your parents and mine, would have helped us to reach adulthood without most of the hang-ups we've acquired.

Train up a child in the way he should go: and when he is old, he will not depart from it.

Proverbs 22:6

Many of our parents did not train us in the way we should go. This includes everything involved in child training. This is the responsibility of parents as God sees it. But we have already said that we are all imperfect people, so let's not be too harsh on our parents. You may not do as well raising your own children. But hopefully, you will do a better job.

Sometimes a child is not trained in the way he should go because parents do not know how to do this. If parents are too wrapped up with their own problems, they are not likely to be sensitive to the needs of their children. Sometimes one or both parents have died and the child has been raised by others who have not been qualified. Some children are placed in foster homes and moved from family to family while they are young, never experiencing the security of a permanent family relationship and never staying long enough with one family to be significantly influenced towards mature behavior, even if the foster parents were equipped to teach them. A chronically-ill parent who requires a lot of time from the other parent can deprive a child of significant learning experiences, also.

In addition to the influence of parents, we are affected more than we may realize, both as children and adults, by other members of the family, home surroundings, school experiences, associations with friends, and other factors.

Perhaps you have not learned how to think and behave in a mature manner because of some of these factors we have mentioned, or perhaps for some other reason. But you can begin where you are, accepting yourself as a person whom God loves, and go on from there to learn what you have not learned before.

HOW OTHERS SEE YOU—
HOW YOU SEE YOURSELF

One way to get to know yourself is to use an information sheet similar to the one on page 75. It would be helpful for you to sit down and candidly evaluate your strengths and weaknesses from your perspective. Follow this up by making a list of changes you would like to see in yourself.

It would also be valuable for you to get a candid evaluation of your strengths and weaknesses from members of your family and other people who know you well. You could give each of them a form similar to the one found on page 76.

Let's say that your name is Sally. Write in Sally where it says name on page 75. Also write in Sally on the line in the middle of the page.

When you give out a form such as the one on page 76 to someone else for evaluation have them put their name on the top and your name in the blanks below. After you have compiled all of the information from all of the forms you have handed out, make a complete list of areas where you need to improve. A sample form is found on page 77.

When you put your name on the top of the page you are entering a contract with yourself and every other week you should sit down and candidly assess whether or not you have improved, putting in the appropriate code letter. After a period of time your marks should be mostly *M*s and you'll know you're going in the right direction. Your ability to receive constructive criticism and act on it is a sign of maturity.

When you read the results of these forms you should have a better understanding of the kind of person you really are. KNOW ALL YOU CAN ABOUT YOURSELF. Why? Too often people have untapped resources — unknown gifts and abilities. We tend to play them down. We also close our eyes to our own imperfections, or blow them up out of all proportion.

HOW IT BEGINS

In the process of growing up a kid wants to feel confident, to accomplish something. Suppose Mom and Dad have just come from the store. There are bags of groceries in the car on the back seat. Their little three-year-old son runs to the driveway where the car is being unloaded and grabs and holds a big bag twice his size. He struggles to keep it from falling while he shouts, "Hey, look at me! I'm helping." What he really is saying is something like this: "I want you to praise me. I want to feel like a worthwhile member of the family."

But perhaps Dad, out of regard for the groceries, takes the bag from him and says, "That bag is too big for you. You might drop it." Translated into terms the child can understand it comes across like, "You're inadequate. You're not good enough to carry that bag." Some parents are even more direct with their admonitions. "Put it down. Do you want to waste all that money I spent on groceries by dropping them?" A

better approach would have been for the father or
mother to say "Boy! Am I proud of you. Thanks a lot
for wanting to help me with the groceries," at the same
time taking them from him.

This father has reacted imperfectly to what his
child attempted to do; and in turn the child will react
imperfectly to his father's outburst, interpreting it as
an evaluation that he is worthless, inferior, and inadequate. These inferiority feelings will continue to
plague him into adulthood unless he understands how
they came about. If you have inferiority feelings based
on imperfect reactions to some childhood experience
you need to realize, first, that these negative evalua-
tions that you have allowed to lodge in your mind are
lies. You *are* worth something. It is not egotistical or
sinful to hold the concept, "I am a worthwhile person."

GOD'S EVALUATION

Many Christians do not appropriate God's evaluation of them as His sons and joint heirs with Christ.
The following should be used whenever you find those
negative thoughts surfacing, to counteract the debilitating effects:

*We feel worthless because we think we are. Negative
feelings flow from negative thoughts.*

This comes from being treated negatively. The remedy
for such a situation is to think TRUTH instead of
FALSITY. For example: "I need to have a feeling of

peace and well-being to help me go through life operating effectively on all levels. I like the person I am becoming because I believe I am loved by God. Jesus loved me so much that He died for me. That demonstrates that I am a worthwhile person, because God loves me, and anybody whom God loves I mustn't be afraid to love." Then we transfer the focus of our thinking to God and away from self.

RETALIATION

Suppose you make it difficult for people to reach you. You're curt. You clam up. You don't open yourself up because you want to see how much effort others will exert to break your shell. You get angry if they don't. You behave like this because your goal is to make others feel guilty. If you feel hurt or neglected you will say something to make others feel guilty, and this will make them pay for what they did to you.

Now the above is a violation of the biblical exhortation to speak the *truth* in love. If you're not being honest with people, if you're playing the guilt game, then you're not expressing Christ's personality, especially his humility.

FREEDOM TO FAIL

God created Adam and Eve and put them in a perfect environment. He gave them free choice. And they failed. Likewise, parents must give their children free choices as God does, in order to propel them towards maturity. But if they have given them a sense of love, of importance, of belonging, and then the child fails when he or she is given free choice, the parent must not feel guilt if he goes astray. The obstacle to raising perfect children is our own imperfections.

The parable of the prodigal son (Luke 15:11–32) is often alluded to as an example of how God deals with His errant children. The father in the parable is seen as a good father. He represents God. Presumably this father is also a model of how fathers ought to be. But this great man had problems with both of his sons. The one became an outcast, the other a self-righteous snob. But this father is not reprimanded for the failures of his sons. Presumably, he did his best to bring them up well. If their innate selfishness and strong wills led each of them into sins of different sorts, this can't be charged against their father. I hope neither of these sons represents your behavior.

ARE YOU CHEATING YOURSELF?

Over and over again, people cheat themselves in some very important aspect of their lives by not understanding themselves and not getting help sooner. As an example let's look into the life of a nineteen-year-old youth who had cheated himself.

Gary and his sister lived in a family situation that looked to those on the outside like a happy family unit. But they were far from happy. Ever since Gary could remember he and his sister had been taken to Sunday school and church by his mother. His father didn't ever go to church. At home they were drilled in memorizing Bible verses. Their mother did most of the disciplining, often accompanied by dire threats of what God would do to them for disobeying. Gary and his sister grew up to have a concept of God that was like a big policeman in the sky, waiting to pounce on them for the slightest infraction of rules. The atmosphere in the home was one of tenseness. As these youngsters were growing up their mother would yell and scream at them when they missed a Bible club meeting, if they didn't memorize their Scripture correctly, or if they forgot to say their prayers. She was a strict disciplinarian in all areas, but in spiritual things she seemed to be particularly touchy.

When Gary was thirteen he went forward at a camp meeting to supposedly accept Jesus Christ as his Saviour. But he was frank to admit to me that he didn't really have any idea of committing his life to Christ at all; it was a case of going forward because most of the other kids did. Also, his mother had warned him before he left that there would be a campfire meeting and she expected him to go forward at it and come home very much changed for the better.

Now he was eighteen and had been attending Sunday school and church for fifteen of those years. He was antagonistic and rebellious towards his mother. He confided that he went through the motions of being a Christian, sat in the class, answered the questions, and memorized the Scripture, but that when he was honest with himself it was just an act. Recently, he said some of the things he had studied about God in creation had gotten through to him and he wondered if perhaps there might not be validity to the claims of Christ that He was man's only way to God. But he usually put such thoughts out of his mind as soon as they surfaced. "I wouldn't give her the satisfaction," he said. I suggested he ask himself the following questions (whenever you react in a negative way it might be well for you to copy these questions on a card and write out your own answers):

1. Why do I feel this way?
2. What am I reacting to?
3. Are there other factors involved that I'm not even aware of?
4. Do I know the whole picture behind my reactions?
5. What more could I do?

This was the kind of problem that involved the whole family. Gary's answers indicated that he knew very little about why his mother might have behaved the way she did. His sister had rebelled openly and cut herself loose from the family when she went to college. They seldom saw her. His father busied himself with his profession and was seldom home. When he was there he stayed out of the way as much as possible and said little.

We decided to interview his mother next and then have a family conference with everyone attending, if they would agree. Gary's mother came to see me, not because she thought she had a problem, but because she thought she could tell me some more about her son's rebellious spirit. But in the course of the interviews we found the answer to her children's rebellion and her husband's withdrawn behavior.

Gary's mother had become a Christian in her teens. She had married an unbeliever, against the wishes of her parents and the convictions of her own conscience. She knew she had sinned deliberately. She asked God to forgive her but she didn't take Him at His word—and she couldn't forgive herself. So for the rest of her married life she was governed by the unconscious need to make atonement to God for her failure to marry a Christian. The only way she felt she could do this was to be a superior mother in every respect, especially when it came to seeing that her children obeyed the God whom she had offended.

When she understood her motivation and what she had done to herself, her husband (who certainly wasn't motivated by her behavior to love Christ), and her children, she was appalled. Self-discovery and self-understanding helped her to change. But it took several years and lots of reliance on the Holy Spirit. At the family conference she told her husband and children what had been behind her behavior and asked for their understanding and forgiveness.

When Gary and I talked together again he was better able to assess his problem of rebellion. Some of it had drained away in the process of understanding the unconscious motivation for his mother's behavior. But he realized that he needed to turn his thoughts frequently to the Holy Spirit for help in guarding against the growth of resentment for the years of his unhappy childhood.

I was also able to help Gary to see how he had cheated himself by refusing to yield to the claims of Christ. For the pleasure of withholding something from his mother—in an effort to be vindictive—he had been willing to sacrifice his opportunity to become a child of God. For the pleasure of hurting the one who had hurt him, he had been willing to sentence himself to an eternity without Christ. He realized then that he was paying too high a price for the satisfaction of getting even and he yielded his life to Christ. Today he is a spirit-controlled Christian with a positive witness among young people.

I want you to carefully consider if you might be in any respect like Gary. Use the question card and think and pray about your situation. Perhaps the solution to an unhappy home lies with your willingness to take the initiative. Parents are often willing to talk to an objective person like a professional counselor. Frequently they are puzzled by their own behavior but they don't know how to get help.

THE ENEMY IN HIDING

One of the most important steps you can take toward understanding yourself is to have a thorough physical examination. Many individuals who seem to have emotional problems, whose behavior causes unpleasant reactions in themselves and others, are in reality displaying the symptoms of a physical disorder of some kind. There are many illnesses which can affect the individual's attitudes and behavior in various ways. One abnormal condition that often exists without the individual being aware of it is hypoglycemia, or low blood sugar. I have seen dramatic changes in individuals who had come to me for counseling because they had frequent spells of free-floating anxiety — a feeling as if something terrible was going to happen. Some of these people were subject to frequent crying spells or temper tantrums. Others seemed to be moody and irritable. Some had periods of restlessness or unexplainable phobias.

Rod was one of those people. He was in his twenties, engaged, and looking forward to marriage. He was a science teacher in one of the local schools and enjoyed what he was doing. While he and Judy were dating, before the engagement, she had some reservations about continuing the relationship, but she accepted his ring and then they came to me for counseling. "Rod is a great person," she confided, "but sometimes he changes abruptly. He gets into an argument over some silly little thing and loses his temper. Then he takes me home and leaves in a sulk. Lots of times it's a dinner date he's broken while we're on the way to the restaurant. After he drops me off at home he drives somewhere to get a hamburger. I guess then he feels sorry. So he calls me up and apologizes and asks me to get ready and we'll go out for a dinner after all. By that time I've usually eaten a sandwich already. And anyway, I'm mad at him after he's acted like such a kid, so I won't go."

When I questioned Rod he was at a loss to explain his sudden irritability with Judy at certain times. But when I asked him to try to recall if there was any pattern to the timing of these incidents, he seemed to feel that they usually happened when he and Judy were planning on a late dinner date at a restaurant that required a fairly long drive from home. This alerted me to the possibility of some medical problem involving a blood-sugar-level imbalance and I suggested that he have a complete checkup before he came back for additional conferences. His physician administered a glucose tolerance test as part of the examination and the results indicated that Rod suffered from functional hypoglycemia. His blood-sugar level dropped to an abnormal low three hours after the administration of glucose. Accompanying this low sugar level in the blood were signs of the jitters, restlessness, weakness, irritability, and some anxiety. These were the same symptoms that appeared when he had a dinner date with Judy and didn't eat until more than four hours after his previous meal. The quick hamburger and milk he invariably ate on the way home after an argument and breaking the date with Judy raised his blood sugar to a normal level within a few minutes. Then he felt his anger subside, his irritability had gone, and he would telephone his apology. But Rod had never connected his change of mind with eating a meal. If he hadn't gone to a physician for a thorough checkup the troublesome condition might never have been discovered. Rod would have been tagged as "unpredictable" and "quick tempered" because of something over which he had no control. And he might have lost

Judy, too, or made their marriage a difficult and frustrating one.

So if you are going to make a serious effort to understand yourself as a prerequisite to becoming a good marriage partner, make an appointment with a well-qualified doctor for a thorough physical examination. If you decide to have individual counseling as part of your effort at self-understanding, or premarriage counseling with your partner, you will find this to be a worthwhile investment.

QUESTIONS FOR DISCUSSION

1. What correlation is there between understanding yourself and a happy marriage relationship?
2. What is involved in understanding yourself?
3. How can a person's physical health affect his marriage?

3

You Can Change

People are interested in things that work. I am interested in things that work, and God's Word has *worked* in my life. For many years I felt inferior and insecure, but God changed my life. Although my destiny was changed, according to God's Word, at the instant of my conversion, the process of changing my self-image and attitudes was only begun then. Change implies growth, and that's what happened to me.

For if a man is in Christ he becomes a new person altogether—the past is finished and gone, everything has become fresh and new.

2 Corinthians 5:17 PHILLIPS

As newborn babes, desire the sincere milk of the word, that ye may grow thereby.

1 Peter 2:2

YOUR IDENTITY

To become a well-adjusted person, everyone needs a healthy sense of identity. By identity I mean an answer to the seemingly trite question, Who am I?

As far as God is concerned He has, along with physical life, given each one of us an identity. According to the ninth chapter of Hebrews we are individuals whom God loves. God has named you as a beneficiary to receive forgiveness of your sins and eternal life, making you a member of God's family if you accept that inheritance. However, many people either haven't known how potentially wealthy they are, or have refused this legacy.

How many Christians do you know who are tremendously happy because they are members of God's family? Because someday they will live eternally with Him? Probably not too many. Instead they are preoccupied with physical, intellectual, social, and economic concerns and with their own abilities and endowments or lack of them. They don't give serious thought to the tremendous resource they have as Christians—the knowledge that God loves them. This should give a person a great feeling of security and inner peace. This knowledge can help a person weather the storms he may have in his life.

God has given you the most satisfying identity you could have. If you do not experience this gratifying sense of identity it may be because you haven't known about it, or because you haven't chosen to have it.

We are all eternal beings who have come into existence as a result of the operation of God's law of reproduction. This physical existence is not an end in itself, however. No matter what heritage we have been given, we have the opportunity to make a choice that is solely ours — the opportunity to accept or reject the Creator of the universe. This choice determines whether in the life to come we are to be with God, or eternally separated from Him.

Realistically speaking, everyone is *not* born equal. We do not all have equal chances in life. It is a sign of good mental health when we can accept that fact, that our life chances may not be as good as others. We have not been born with the physical, social, financial, or emotional endowment that someone else has been born with. A person with a good sense of identity realizes that he is in the situation he finds himself in because of certain biological and social factors.

YOUR CHOICE

I feel that a well-adjusted person, regardless of his endowment or background, is one who has accepted himself as a person whom God loves. He is pleased with the emotional and spiritual growth taking place in his life as a result of his friendship with the Creator. In addition he is becoming a nice person. What does that mean? He accepts you. He is a person you can be confidential with and know that He will not betray your trust. He has come to realize that he cannot change his endowments, and he *can* choose to be a nice person. He may not be handsome, or talented in art or music or athletics or speech, the way some people are. But he can be a nice person. He can be loyal, dependable, and sensitive to others. He can be nonthreatening and fun to be with. He can be the kind of person who says, "I like knowing that God loves me very much and, therefore, I can like myself. I like people and people feel comfortable with me because I don't need to use them to make me feel happy. God makes me feel important and happy."

Until you feel that you have a healthy sense of identity, life will have little meaning for you. A teenager whom I am counseling tries to get drunk every day because he feels life has no meaning. Another young person said to me, "I feel like I was born in a drawer and have lived my whole life there. I have a shut-away feeling; cut off from other people." He also feels that life is meaningless and has turned to drugs as an escape from that feeling.

Some people become involved in a pattern of promiscuous sex as an escape. Many people are constantly on the go or fixed in front of a TV so that they will not have to face up to the fact that life has little meaning for them. Much of the Christian's unhappiness comes from a faulty relationship with God and violating biblical principles. The unhappy non-Christian is unhappy because he has a faulty relationship with other people, and no relationship at all with God. Both kinds of people are looking for an escape from the boredom of meaninglessness.

Good mental health includes accepting the fact

that as a human being you are not going to perform
perfectly. Just having been born into this world will
mean that you are already defective. But you need to
evaluate yourself to know how defective you are and to
prevent the defectiveness from crippling you. It will
be difficult enough for you to have a reasonably happy
marriage without taking on unnecessary problems. If
you and your intended mate are not working to make
your relationship happy, then your marriage will
probably come apart and you may not even be aware of
the reasons why.

To a certain extent you may not have had much
control over certain aspects of your character and behavior up to this time. But you must accept the fact that
you now have responsibility for and power over your
personality and actions.

If you don't change, it's because you don't really
want to, not because you can't. Usually people don't
want to endure the emotional pain involved in changing. There are three ways in which people react to
negative situations and relationships.

1. Rebellion. This is the reaction that many immature persons respond with because it is the way of
   least resistance. It doesn't require thought. The
   person reacts with anger. Or if he is still living
   under the parental roof, he may indulge in all
   sorts of behavior that the parents disapprove of,
   just so that he can show that he is a free agent.
   But such a person isn't really free because he is at
   the mercy of his temper. He behaves negatively

   to prove his independence from parental control.
2. Another way to react is to choke down your negative feelings. The person doesn't let them surface
   to his consciousness so that he won't feel guilty.
   Sometimes these negative feelings breed resentment and may fester, becoming like a disease that
   damages the body.
3. The third way of reacting, and the only one that
   will produce positive results, is to behave in a
   mature way, accepting and putting into practice
   the biblical principle that applies to the situation.
   This kind of reaction promotes the growth of a
   person emotionally and spiritually.

Many people *want* to change but do not. They have
the desire but the motivation is lacking. For example,
a chubby fiancée was a source of exasperation to her
husband-to-be because she wouldn't diet and kept making excuses for herself. Until—the "chubby" learned
that her future husband's former girl friend, who had
broken her engagement to him for a modeling career,
was coming to town for a visit in a month. Do I need
to tell you that she went on a diet and lost all of her
extra pounds? The secret? *Motivation!* Some people
don't change until they are faced with a crisis.

YOUR RESPONSIBILITY

Don't make the mistake of hiding your deficiencies. Own up to them and be willing to do something

about them. Try to understand how they came about. Usually it can be traced to the failure of your parents plus your own immature reaction to the way you were brought up. But don't make the mistake of using them as a cop-out for continuing in this state for the rest of your life.

Up until now you may have legitimately felt that you are largely the product of experiences and relationships over which you had little or no control. But from now on you are the one who will be responsible for what you are. What happened to you is over with. Accept that. You can rise above your negative conditioning of the past and become the person you really want to be. It is how you react to what has happened to you that will determine your future happiness. For example, a child who suffers a deformed leg because of a parent's carelessness in backing out of the garage can sulk through life, blaming his parent for his handicap. He can become a self-pitying, resentful, and unhappy person who will not get far in this world. Or he can decide that now that he is a young adult and understands how accidents can happen, he will consciously forgive his parent, wipe the slate clean, evaluate his plus characteristics and launch a career that doesn't require that he have two perfect legs.

If you have been emotionally crippled, you have the same choices. Forgive, forget the past, evaluate your present, and work with a positive attitude towards your future. You may need skilled help to modify some of your emotional scars and evaluate your potential. Your counselor and your pastor can be helpful allies but God, through His Holy Spirit, is your greatest source of your power to change.

BASIC STEPS TO HELP YOU

Evaluate the kind of person you have become by asking yourself the following questions:

1. How do I approach difficulties and personal problems? Do I bring into play defense or escape mechanisms?
2. How independent in thought and action am I?
3. Do I possess self-confidence or inferiority feelings, feelings of rejection or acceptance, a sense of security or insecurity?
4. What is my basic attitude toward myself?
5. What are my attitudes towards others? Am I critical or accepting? Do I basically like or dislike, trust or distrust people?
6. What is my attitude toward sex, marriage, children, members of the opposite sex and myself as a member of my own sex?
7. What is my philosophy of life? Christ-centered or nonreligious, optimistic or pessimistic?
8. Am I capable of giving and receiving mature love?

IT'S NOT TOO LATE

Every one of you has a picture of yourself as a person, a self-image, fixed deeply in your mind. The concept you have of yourself may be accurate or false, but your mind does not distinguish for you. It accepts the picture you have handed it and then motivates you to act in accordance with that image. If your concept is that of a pleasant, confident person, you will be inclined to have a good disposition and to make the most of your talents and opportunities because you *believe* that is the kind of person you are. On the other hand, if you visualize yourself as a failure, worthless and unlovable, as someone who "never gets the breaks," you will find yourself putting things off, neglecting opportunities, and making poor judgments, because these are the kinds of things a failure does and your behavior is consistent with the image you have of yourself. The Bible propounded the theory of self-image psychology centuries ago, "For as he thinketh in his heart, so is he . . ." (Proverbs 23:7)

When you are a child your self-image is not yet fully formed. It is developed and added to and modified by your experiences until it becomes, in maturity, a full portrait of the kind of person you believe yourself to be. A girl usually bases her idea of what women are like and, therefore, the kind of person she will become, on the impressions she gets from her mother. A boy is similarly affected by his father. Both are particularly influenced by the attitudes and behavior of the parent with whom they identify.

But what happens when children haven't had adequate models? Is there any hope for them? I do not believe that people are merely the pawns of fate and circumstance. I am convinced that the negative effects of having had inadequate models are not irreversible. We have the freedom to change our behavior. I have seen it happen in the lives of many of those who have come to me for counseling, and I have seen it in my own life.

There are many causes for a poor self-image; for a feeling of meaninglessness to living and therefore a lack of direction to a person's life. Often the reasons for these feelings lie buried in the past and the help of a trained counselor is necessary to uncover them. Once that is done, the process of change can begin.

Often I am asked exactly what kind of counseling is given and how long it takes. This is almost like asking if a hypothetical individual with an undiagnosed illness goes to a doctor, how long will it take to cure him? Each person is a unique individual with a background and characteristics that differ from anyone else's. It is impossible to generalize. But the important thing is that people *can* change. The willingness of the person to have that change take place is basic to the solution of the problem. If you are a Christian, the unlimited power of God through the Holy Spirit is available to you for guidance and for strength. And in addition you have the privilege of communicating with God Himself about your needs in that meditative activity called prayer.

> For the spirit that God gave us is no craven spirit, but one to inspire strength, love, and self-discipline.
>
> 2 Timothy 1:7 NEB

MODELS

A young couple came to me recently for help. They had been married for less than a year and they were on the verge of divorce. Everyone had said that they were suited to each other and that theirs would be an ideal marriage. During the time they were dating, Jane behaved as though she thought Greg was a wise and wonderful guy. She asked his advice about many things and she seemed to be proud of his advancement with his company.

But as soon as they were married she began to show a side of her personality that Greg hadn't realized existed. She told him what to do and how to do it and was disagreeable until she got her way. She belittled him before guests and seldom complimented him on anything, including his business accomplishments. When Greg couldn't stand it any longer he called me for an appointment, but Jane refused to come with him. Only when Greg told her he would move out of their home if she wasn't willing to cooperate did she agree to an appointment.

After questioning them separately, I discovered that Jane was acting out the pattern of marriage she had seen in her own home. Her model was her mother. During her growing-up years she had unconsciously absorbed the idea that in marriage the woman dominates the man, just as her mother had dominated her father. Jane was surprised and upset when she realized what she had been doing and why. But she loved her husband and was willing to try to change her behavior.

We worked out a plan sheet for her (page 77) so that she could rate herself every day on how well she had done. It gave her a sense of accomplishment when she could report progress. The attitudes acquired over a period of years can't be changed in a matter of weeks, but Jane's and Greg's relationship improved so much after several months that divorce became unthinkable to them. Jane had had an inadequate model during childhood on which to pattern her adult behavior, but the effects were not unalterable and she has proved it.

PEACE

Thou wilt keep him in perfect peace, whose mind is stayed on thee. . . .

Isaiah 26:3

We must saturate our lives with God's Word. We must take advantage of God's status and our relationship as His children. God is a difficult concept to relate to. Fathers and mothers form their concepts of God and try to instill these thoughts in their children. What they often do not realize is that their children think of God as an authority figure similar in many respects to the most important authority figure in their lives, their father. This is a sobering thought and one that ought to make us more than ever conscious of the responsibilities of parenthood.

HOW TO CHANGE

Parents rarely see their children as being worthless, even though they may treat the children in such a
way, and speak in such a way that the child gets that
impression. This may be their way of instilling in their
sons and daughters a desire to do better. Parents may
mistakenly feel that the way to teach children to be
responsible and mature is to constantly point out their
faults. In rearing their own children, parents tend to
reproduce the way they've been brought up by their
parents. And their own parents may have constantly
criticized them. They assume that their children know
that this is their motivation. But they do not realize that
praise and compliments would be more of an incentive
than constant nagging.

Unfortunately you can't undo these unhealthy,
erroneous comments that your parents may have made.
But you can change the way you are reacting to those
comments, whether they made them when you were
younger or whether they're still making these comments.

You have two alternatives when you hear or remember negative comments about yourself:

1. You can assume that the comments are true, that
   you are a failure and worthless.
2. You can accept the fact that your parents may have
   been well intentioned, but that they chose a
   method of improving your behavior that was

harmful and that led you to erroneous conclusions about yourself.

If you do not decide to change, then you are likely to become the kind of parent who will foster an unhealthy emotional climate in your own home. Your own children will grow up with the same problems in self-image that you have because you, as a parent, have unrealistic expectations of yourself and them.

So in order to begin to change, you will need to acknowledge that your parents were sincere but wrong in the way they acted and you were sincere but wrong in the way you reacted. Unless this vicious cycle stops with you, it will go on and on for generations. The following is an example of how walls develop between parents and children.

The words that you hear from your parents hurt you. To avoid that hurt you tend to avoid contact with them. This rejection hurts them. They may interpret your aloofness as disrespect or ingratitude. Often they react with phrases like, "After all we've done for you. . . ."

Sometimes the child acts out his hurt by rebelling against the parents in anger. Whether the child withdraws or rebels openly, both are unsatisfactory ways of reacting.

The kids, realizing the sincerity and other good aspects of the parents, feel guilty about hurting them. Feeling guilty reinforces their feeling of worthlessness. The child may tend to feel that the only way he can be accepted by his parents is to perform perfectly. But since he cannot achieve perfection, he may feel he is a constant disappointment to his parents.

Now a *little* child is defenseless against the constant criticism of his parents. He is not mature enough to be able to separate truth from error. He reacts by believing that he is worthless because he doesn't know any better. BUT YOU ARE NOT A CHILD. You may still be reacting like an immature child out of habit, but I want to teach you how to react in a mature manner so that you can change to be the kind of person who is not a prisoner of false ideas.

There is another option open to you. There is a biblical principle involved here.

> No, let us speak the truth in love; so shall we fully grow up in Christ.
>
> Ephesians 4:15 NEB

Let your parents know that you are bleeding emotionally. Of course, it would be nice if the parents would get insight, being impressed by your maturity, and make a step toward you. But many times you must take this first step.

Some find such a confrontation with their parents easy; with others it is difficult. Some feel that such a heart-to-heart talk would be undesirable because of the parents' poor health and the guilt they would feel if the parents had a negative physical reaction—or because they know that one or both parents are stubborn, proud, and inclined to behave unreasonably in such a situation.

DECISIONS

If your parents will not listen to you, if they behave unreasonably, or if you think it wiser not to confront them, then you must be prepared to assume the responsibility of changing your attitude about yourself without any help from them. Your relationship with Christ must become the dominant one in your life, as it should be, only now you will see that that relationship stands to suffer when you continue to let a granite-like personality promote continuous bleeding in your emotional life. Your relationship with Christ should be strong enough so that Christ can serve as your healer whenever you suffer emotional pain.

But what if the emotional damage is continuous and severe from an irrational, unreasonable, tyrannical parent? Then you must be completely honest in evaluating the damage to your personality and emotional health in the light of your relationship to Christ and your obligation to follow His will for your life.

If you can cope with such a difficult parent relationship, this is fine. Human beings have survived concentration camps and other almost unbearable circumstances and have come out on top as better people. They were able to accept their difficult circumstances as a challenge. And I would urge this as a first choice of action. But if trying this approach is unsatisfactory, if you find that staying in such circumstances is making you an emotional cripple and damaging your ability to follow God's will for your life, then you must honestly face this question and answer it: *Does my relationship with my parents come before my relationship with Christ?*

Any professional counselor would concur that in many cases a child's worst enemies have been his parents. Even Jesus said, ". . . a man will find his enemies under his own roof. No man is worthy of me who cares more for father or mother than for me . . ." (Matthew 10:36, 37 NEB).

If you are mature and responsible, then your only satisfactory alternative may be to leave your home and live somewhere else. This, of course, will involve stress situations both before and after you move, but that is the price you will have to pay. Whether or not this is the most satisfactory answer for you may not be easy to determine, and I would strongly advise that you get some competent counseling before undertaking such a step. If your parents will agree to family counseling this would help all of you to come to a reasonable course of action.

But whatever you decide to do, you will certainly need Jesus Christ as your Lord in order to cope.

". . . for without me ye can do nothing" (John 15:5). His strength flowing through us produces fruit in our lives. Stressful times are like pruning a vine, they soon pass and are good for us. If I had to choose between the pruning times in my life and the increasing fruitfulness of my life from then on, or avoiding the pruning and therefore the fruitfulness, I would choose the former, painful though it is.

Principles for Personal, Marital, and Family Mental Health

1. Obey Jesus' command to love yourself. Before you can have a healthy self-love you need to be freed from guilt feelings and remorse. You can do this:

By accepting the fact that God loves you.

> Thou shalt not avenge, nor bear any grudge against the children of thy people, but thou shalt love thy neighbour as thyself: I am the Lord.
>
> Leviticus 19:18

By accepting His forgiveness.

> I write to you, my children, because your sins have been forgiven for his sake.
>
> 1 John 2:12 NEB

By accepting His inheritance of eternal life.

> The witness is this: that God has given us eternal life, and that this life is found in his Son.
>
> 1 John 5:11 NEB

By accepting His promise to be with you as you try to live your life for Him.

> I have been crucified with Christ: the life I now live is not my life, but the life which

Christ lives in me; and my present bodily
life is lived by faith in the Son of God, who
loved me and sacrificed himself for me.

> Galatians 2:20 NEB

2. Acknowledge the truth of:

. . . he that winneth souls is wise.

> Proverbs 11:30

Be wise by sharing your inheritance of eternal
life with others.

3. In seeking a mate, choose a spiritually growing
Christian (as you hopefully are) rather than a
nongrowing one. Don't marry a spiritual dwarf.
In close association they are more apt to pull you
down, to stunt your spiritual growth, than you are
to influence them to grow.

Do not unite yourselves with unbelievers;
they are no fit mates for you . . . .

> 2 Corinthians 6:14 NEB

4. Leave your parents.

Therefore shall a man leave his father and his
mother, and shall cleave unto his wife: and
they shall be one flesh.

> Genesis 2:24

Cut your umbilical cords and establish an identity, life-style, and family unit of your own.

5. Know yourself through personal counseling, if necessary.

6. Establish leadership in the home. So many men are not prepared to become the spiritual head of the home, so they can't carry out the job. If a man is willing, he can learn from his wife, from books, from professionals. He can train to be a spiritual leader just as men in business, politics, and the military learn to be leaders.

7. Touch. Learn the importance of touching. Jesus touched people when He healed them and at other times. The prodigal's father embraced and kissed him. Children who grow up without close physical contact with their parents suffer emotional damage.

Steps to Help You

1. Evaluate the kind of person you have become (by studying questionnaires filled out by you, your intended mate, parents and other relatives, friends, your minister, co-workers, organization associates).

2. Understand, where possible, how you got that way (preferably by getting trained help from a counselor, minister, etc.).

3. Acknowledge the need to change some things about yourself, and make a list of them.

4. Be realistic. Recognize that you cannot go back and change what has happened to you in the past. You do not have to be a prisoner to the past. You can change. Many thousands of people do change. You can become the person you want to be. Get competent counseling to help you.

5. In response to Christ's directive, forgive those who may have been responsible for the undesirable thought patterns, attitudes, or behavior which you would like to change. Forgive them, whether their negative influences on you were caused by ignorance or intention.

6. Ask God to forgive you for any resentment that you may have developed towards people or circumstances that have influenced you negatively. Ask Him to replace the spirit of bitterness with His love.

7. By a definite act of your will, turn over the matter of your self-improvement to God. Trust Him to help you achieve your goals through the power of the Holy Spirit.

8. If you are going steady with the one you plan to marry, ask him or her to take these basic steps, also. Help and encourage each other as you work to change your negative qualities to more desirable ones.

9. Evaluate your progress at the end of each week, using the chart on page 75 as a guide.

LIST OF POSITIVE AND NEGATIVE TRAITS

Name: _____   Date: _____

What I like about myself	What I don't like about myself

I, _____, need to work on the following: Date: _____

_____

_____

_____

_____

_____

_____

_____

_____

_____

_____

_____

_____

_____

LIST OF POSITIVE AND NEGATIVE TRAITS

Name: _____   Date: _____

What I like about _____	What I don't like about _____

I would like _____ to work on the following:

_____

_____

_____

_____

_____

_____

_____

_____

_____

_____

_____

WORK TO DO AT HOME

CODE: M = MUCH IMPROVEMENT
         S = SLIGHT IMPROVEMENT
         N = NO IMPROVEMENT

I, _____ , agree to do the following:

	Date	Evaluation				

QUESTIONS FOR DISCUSSION

1. How does one develop a healthy sense of identity?
2. How can a person go about changing a negative trait in his personality?
3. What are some typical problems that a person needs to resolve before he should enter a marriage relationship?

4

Communication

NEEDS

There is never going to be a perfect marriage. You and your mate will always have needs to be met and these needs are often in the process of change. Marriage is not a static state, but is fluid—ebbing and flowing, changing and growing. Those needs can be met by each of you, but you have to know about them first, and that is why it is so important to learn to communicate.

SOUND AND TOUCH

Communication begins early in life, before a child learns to talk. If our parents spoke to us calmly, in soft tones, we felt secure and loved. But a child can become insecure by hearing shouting and screaming and some of your insecurity may stem from such experiences when you were very young. Communication came to us as infants through sounds; harsh sounds frightened us, soft sounds soothed us. Messages came to us through the way we were handled. Arms that held us securely transmitted a message that said, "You're safe"; arms that held us tensely like a bomb that might explode at any moment, carried the signal that "this person isn't sure of himself," and we experienced insecurity. Quick, impatient, or rough handling instantly communicated the emotion of fear and we reacted by crying.

From the moment of birth, *we* began to communicate too, often at odd hours of the day and night. We cried when we were hungry, thirsty, wet, uncomfortable, irritable, frightened, and often for reasons which were obscure to our parents.

LEARNING

Now the kinds of communication we've talked about are instinctive. We didn't have to be taught to cry. And those who held us and attended to our needs transmitted their emotions to us without conscious forethought. But a world in which communication remained on that level would be hard to visualize. We all had to *learn* to communicate effectively. Some of us were apt pupils and learned quickly; others were slow; and still others have never learned. There are some people who have mastered the art of communication, but most of us have a need to improve our communication skills in some areas.

BARRIERS

It may seem strange to say that many couples in love are unable to communicate, but this is one of the chief problems for which people come for counseling. Communication is going on all the time, but what information is being sent and what is being received? Does the receiver get an accurate message or does he misinterpret the message? If he misinterprets the message that was given, is it because it wasn't given clearly or because the receiver has read into the message something that wasn't sent? Problems arise when a faulty message is received and action is taken based on that erroneous message.

Sometimes our communications are given verbally to another; sometimes by an expression on our face or an attitude; sometimes by a stony silence which may convey hostility or indifference. If you listen with angry feelings, that anger will color what you hear. Sometimes wishful thinking colors the message. People hear what they want to hear.

Occasionally you may be thinking something, but it comes out of your mouth wrong. One of the best ways to correct a misinterpreted message is to ask the person who sent it, "Did I hear you say this?" and then repeat in your own words what you thought you heard. It's important to make sure that both you and your future mate correct misunderstood messages before either of you have a chance to start building walls between yourselves, to act as barriers and insulate each of you from the other's attempts at communication.

WORDS ARE POWER

One of the most important things you can learn about communicating is to use the right kind of words to convey your message. Words are more than sounds, they create pictures in our minds, too. Sometimes we respond emotionally to the sound of a word; sometimes to the picture it creates; sometimes to both. "You're lazy!" we may say, and the response is instant resentment. A different approach might be, "I feel that you're a person who would be glad to let other people do your work for you." This leaves the door open for further communication. Perhaps the other person will ask, "Why do you say that about me?" We have to be careful of sounding dogmatic, accusative, or judgmental. This is like waving a red flag in front of a bull—it signals trouble.

NEVER

There are two phrases that ought to be dropped from the vocabulary of every couple, unless they are followed by a compliment. This applies whether you are dating, are engaged, or married.

1. You *never* . . . .
2. You *always* . . . .

Perhaps you find it difficult to be on time. In your family being on time was not considered an important virtue. Your future mate comes from a family who considered being punctual the epitome of good character habits. One night your date meets you at the door with the words, "How come you're *never* on time, you're *always* late?" You can feel annoyance building, or outright anger. You become defensive. You hate to be accused of *never* being on time. You must have been on time once in awhile. So it's unfair for the other person not to at least give you credit for the times you *were* prompt. This may spoil the whole date. And it isn't likely that you'll be inspired to change your ways.

On the other hand, suppose your date meets you at the door with a cheerful "Hi!" and seems genuinely glad to see you. Later in the evening he or she may say to you, "Honey, there's something I'd like to help you with. I know it must be hard for you to get ready for dates by a certain time, but I enjoy being with you so much that I hate to lose any of that time waiting for you. Is there something I could do to help you figure out a way to plan your time so that we can both be ready at the same time?" You don't need a marriage counselor to tell you which approach is most likely to succeed.

TABOO

Your marriage will be happier if you learn to eliminate several other phrases from your vocabulary, too, and a good time to start practicing is during the engagement period or even before.

1. You must . . . .
2. You should . . . .
3. You ought to . . . .
4. You're obligated to treat me . . . .

These kinds of phrases are responsible for dissension between individuals and can even wreck a marriage.

Some couples don't realize how uptight their partner feels when he or she announces an opinion as a fact. For instance, Jan sees Bob scowling and says, "You're angry!" "No, I'm *not* angry!" he shouts and the battle is on. Perhaps Bob is disappointed, hurt, puzzled. Any number of emotions could be responsible for his scowl. But if he is accused of being angry when he isn't, he is likely to rebel at Jan's dogmatic approach.

It is wise to get into the habit of wording your opinions so they sound like opinions, and not like certainties. For instance, "I could be wrong, but you appear to be angry." Or, "You seem to me to be angry, but maybe I'm not reading you right."

Although I have tried to show you how words affect our behavior, I don't mean to imply that we should lose all our spontaneity in conversation by weighing each word so carefully before it is spoken. That would make for few conversations and dreadfully dull ones. It is important to have an atmosphere in the parental home that allows the family members to speak freely without fear, including giving and receiving constructive criticism. Misunderstandings can be aired and corrected when the lines of communication are kept open. As you prepare for marriage it is vitally important that you and your partner extend this freedom to communicate to each other, and ultimately to all those who will be part of the new family unit you will establish.

DIFFERENCES

Another aid to learning good communication habits is to remind yourself often that no two people hear the same words in exactly the same way. The meaning of any phrase is colored by the attitude of the speaker, the attitude of the listener, and all of the interaction that has taken place between the two involved. This includes past experiences as well as those immediately preceding the conversation. As an example, let's suppose a TV drama shows an eighteen-year-old youth. He enters a living room in which are sitting his parents, his brother, his sister, his girl friend, and a stranger who is demonstrating a vacuum cleaner. He announces that he has dented the fender of the family's new car. His girl friend jumps up and hurries over to him, concerned about whether or not he has been hurt. His brother and sister glance up momentarily and return their gaze to the football game on TV. The father explodes, "Not again!" It's obvious that his son has been careless with his driving before. The mother sighs and looks resigned. She remembers that he was always an awkward and sometimes careless child from the time he could walk. The salesman is unconcerned. This doesn't involve him at all. Each individual heard the same message: "I dented the fender of the new car," and each one reacted differently to it. It's as though a filter were operating in each mind to color the significance of what was said.

It's especially important to keep this in mind as you learn to communicate with your future mate. His or her background and experiences may have been very different from yours. It takes patience, tact, and sometimes a sense of humor to work through the early attempts at effective communication.

LEARNING TO LISTEN

The art of communication involves listening as well as speaking. Learn to listen actively. Give the speaker your undivided attention. Try to see things through his eyes. Your Bible school lesson may be a boring one for you. Perhaps the teacher is having difficulty stirring up some enthusiasm for the lesson. The temptation is to sit listlessly, thinking about other things, and not paying attention to what is going on. But if you can learn to put yourself in the teacher's place, imagine what is going through his mind as he tries to get the lesson across, then you can develop empathy with that teacher. This will motivate you to search your mind for appropriate questions to ask which will lead to a profitable and perhaps interesting discussion. You can revive interest and boost attendance in a class that is going downhill simply by learning how to listen constructively, one of the most important facets of the art of communication.

Parents are people, too, and they can be persuaded to listen to your viewpoint on something that is very important to you, if you will extend them the courtesy of listening to them — really listening — when they are talking. Some parents are so taken by surprise to find their young people looking at them and listening to them, that they are momentarily caught off guard, and may very well give some serious thought to something they've always given you the brush-off about before. It's worth trying.

Listening attentively to people of all kinds will boost your popularity rating enormously, because there are so few people who are willing to take the time and effort to focus their attention on what another person is saying. One of the fringe benefits of such constructive listening is that you learn a lot about other people — about their thoughts, attitudes, and reactions in stress situations, when most people are motivated to talk as a release from tensions. And as you become an accomplished listener you will find your opportunities to share your faith in Christ increased tremendously. Learning to listen is one of the essential steps in learning to communicate the love of Christ to others because it shows that you care about them.

Learning to listen to the person you hope to marry is a must for a happy marriage. It is possible to sit in the same room with that person you love, and yet be a thousand miles away while you appear to be listening. So prevalent is this kind of behavior that many cartoons and TV comedy routines focus on the preoccupied husband with the newspaper hiding his face, answering yes absentmindedly, only to find that he has gotten himself into some kind of trouble. The serious dating that precedes marriage is the only time you'll ever have to make sure you both are right for each other before you say *I do* and commit yourselves to a marriage relationship. So you will need to learn to listen, to learn as much as you can about this person with whom you expect to spend the rest of your life. If you don't, you may find yourself tied to the wrong partner for you for fifty or more years. That will seem like a life sentence rather than the happy, fulfilling relationship you had anticipated.

QUESTIONS FOR DISCUSSION

1. What is nonverbal communication and how can this kind of communication affect a child?
2. What is meant by the statement, "Words have power to hurt and to heal"?
3. What is involved in good communication and how can one develop this skill?

5

Your Two Biggest Decisions

Decision One—Choosing a Life-style

This book has been aimed primarily toward a Christian readership, but its concepts of mental health and psychological principles apply equally to everyone. It is important for every reader to come to terms with himself, however, to think honestly and earnestly— what is life all about, anyway? Does it have meaning? And if it *has* meaning then there must be some sort of intelligence behind the scenes and the senses.

Now if this intelligence exists, it must be rational. The creative process at work in man and nature defies the imagination in its complexity: in its unity and in its uniqueness. The panorama of sky, mountains, earth, and sea is breathtaking in its grandeur. The geometrical progression evidenced in the arrangements of the petals of a daisy is awesome in its implication.

And so we are led by simple deduction to the conclusion that where there is design there must be a designer. Is it impossible then to believe that it was His energizing power that brought our world and all the worlds we know to being?

If we grant that God exists, that He creates, that He designs, can we not go one step farther and grant the possibility that He loves? And if He loves, who becomes the object of that love? Love that doesn't manifest itself is a strange love indeed. So is it not possible that this Divine Intelligence chose to communicate that love to man?

What better way to show this love than in communication? We have a book, the Bible, in which God communicates His love for man. But man is a rebellious creature and does not take kindly to laws and commandments and precepts. He disobeyed and brought calamity upon himself, and through him to all mankind. God intended a great destiny for the creatures He loved — but the problem of sin stood in the way.

So, God broke into time and space in order to communicate directly and to do this He had to become like one of His creatures and enter His world. This is what Jesus Christ did. Can you imagine the love which prompted the Creator of the universe to be bound by His own laws? The Creator of space and time and worlds seen and unseen, laying aside power that is inconceivable to the mind of man to inhabit an infant's body — the utter humiliation of it?

It is this Jesus Christ of Nazareth who announced His claim to being man's one way to an eternity in the life beyond this. And this is the God-Man who said within minutes of His death on the cross, "Father, forgive them; for they know not what they do" (Luke 23:34).

That the Creator of all universes loves me is an awesome thought. That He died to pay my penalty for every sin I have committed or will commit is staggering. That He arose from death and lives today in a realm beyond the one our senses perceive is mind-boggling. To believe that all we have to do to accept that love and inherit eternal life is to bend our wills to His, bend our heads and hearts and say, "Lord Jesus, I believe You. Come into my life and make me new. Forgive me. Amen." To believe it is this easy takes what we call faith.

Today, if you want to make the decision that will cleanse your conscience from guilt, give you the power to change and become a new person in Christ, give you power to perform your roles more effectively, and especially, help you to become a wise and wonderful mate, then I would recommend that you bow your head wherever you are and bare your soul to Him. Ask Him for forgiveness and accept it. And start a new day tomorrow. A new beginning with a new power.

Decision Two — Choosing a Mate

CHANGING NEEDS

During the late teens and early twenties it is unrealistic to expect that you will have complete personal insight. But you should have enough to enable you to evaluate yourself to some extent. During these years you may be praying that God will help you find a perfect mate, one who will have *every* quality that you could wish for. This is an unrealistic expectation, but you can hope for *many* good qualities. Make a list of the qualities you especially desire in a mate. Then give some thought to those qualities in the light of future years. You may list a strong sexual attraction as one of the desirable qualities, but you may not think to include in that list the qualities of patience and tact which will be important to you ten years from now when you have small children. Or if you are a man, you may include in your list as desirable in a wife, a good sense of fashion and the ability to wear clothes well. But remember to include, too, the traits of thrift and the ability to remain cheerful when she may have to do without some things she would like to have. In your life together there may be some financially lean years, when unusual medical expenses, a child's education, or supplementing an elderly parent's needs make a shambles of your budget.

Look at it this way. Right now you may find that a racing car is just perfect for you. You're single, you're sports-minded, and you have enough money. This car satisfies your needs now. But what about the future? A two-seater won't be big enough when you have a wife and several children, so at that time you'll compromise and buy the best-looking sedan you can find at the price you can afford. The changing years bring changing needs and it may require you to change your attitudes.

RELATIONSHIPS

Sometimes it is changing needs in human relationships that cause problems. A girl who has a miserable homelife has a need and that need is to escape her unpleasant home. At this point she feels she needs protection and will settle for a hasty marriage to a man she knows only slightly who may be inferior to her intellectually and who can provide only for the barest necessities. She is willing to live in a modest apartment, exist on a meager diet, and own few clothes. She'll settle for anything just to get out of her home. So when she marries and lives like this her immediate need has been fulfilled.

But after awhile she outgrows that immediate need and it is replaced by other needs. She may realize that her husband, though he offered her an escape from her intolerable home situation, has deficiencies in other areas that are harder to cope with than what she had to put up with at home. Then she realizes that her most important need at the time she married wasn't to get away—her most important need was to grow up and become a mature and worthwhile person. If the home situation was intolerable, it would have been better for her to get out and live by herself. Then when she was matured, when she has learned to accept responsibility and has become a person in her own right, she can marry a man who is suitable for a lifetime partner and not one who simply offers an escape.

QUALITIES THAT HELP MAKE
A GOOD MARRIAGE

The more alike people are intellectually, ethnically, socially, educationally, athletically, spiritually, etc., the easier their marital adjustment will be.

I'm thinking now in terms of positive qualities. Certainly two stubborn individuals will be compounding their negative qualities. The same could be said for two withdrawn nontalkers, or two compulsive talkers who always want the floor. The old saying that opposites attract may be true but this need not be a barrier to a happy marriage so long as the opposite qualities are in those areas where they will function as complementary to each other, rather than promoting discord, or where the opposite negative quality in one partner is not in a crucial area and can be gradually modified with adequate motivation and understanding. For instance, a rather withdrawn, socially inept man marries an outgoing, friendly woman. In this case if the wife refrains from overwhelming her husband with a constant stream of guests, and invites just one or two couples occasionally for dinner or dessert if he agrees, her husband can be gradually and happily acclimated to a more active social life.

A woman who finds it easy to be systematic and who organizes her time well marries a salesman whose engaging personality and knowledge of his subject gets him orders, but who is at loose ends when it comes to being systematic. She is willing to devote the necessary time to handling this part of his job so that he can be freed to use more time calling on clients.

DANGER SIGNS

Like red lights, blinking danger signs mean *STOP*, then proceed with caution (if at all!). It is better to take this brief test before you become engaged so that if definite danger signs turn up you will have time to do something about them before committing yourself officially to marriage plans. If you are already engaged and encounter danger signs, then by all means delay your wedding plans until you can straighten out the problem areas that you or your partner have. Like icebergs, the negative traits may be hidden from you, and just the tips show what is going on beneath a supposedly mature exterior.

1. A general uneasy feeling about the relationship. Lack of inner peace. A nagging, aching, disturbing feeling inside that says, "Something is wrong." Don't ignore that feeling. It may be your own temporarily numbed common sense, or it may be God's Spirit trying to communicate something to you. More than a few clients have admitted to me that they knew the marriage was a mistake even as they were walking down the aisle.

2. Frequent arguments. Never sure how the date will end. More fighting than fun.

3. Avoiding discussing sensitive subjects because you're afraid of hurting your partner's feelings or starting an argument. You find yourself thinking, "I'd better not talk about this." Perhaps subjects like: "I wish he'd show me more affection, I wish he wouldn't treat his mother so mean. I wonder why he always has a temper tantrum when he gets a flat. Can't he control it better? I wish he would shower more often."

   "She makes a pig of herself when there's a box of candy anywhere in sight—don't you suppose she cares about getting fat? I wish she'd read a book once in a while. Why can't we ever talk about something interesting instead of just superficial topics?"

4. Getting more involved physically. You resolve to limit the acceleration of your physical intimacy, but find that on each new date you start again at the place where you left off. Sometimes couples get involved physically as a way to avoid arguments. Just one of the reasons for this being a danger sign is that your relationship may remain on the physical level only, throughout your courtship and marriage. After you're married you may not like the personality that goes along with the body.

5. If you find yourself always doing what your partner wants you to do. Constantly giving in, being

accommodating. This could indicate a selfish, domineering partner and/or a serious insecurity on your part.

6. If you detect serious emotional disturbances such as extreme fears, extreme shyness, bizarre behavior, irrational anger, inflicting physical injury, inability to demonstrate affection.

7. If you feel you are staying in the relationship through fear. For example, if thoughts like these go through your mind: "I wish I could get out of dating him, but I'm afraid of what he might do to me. Or he might commit suicide. I feel trapped and I couldn't stand the guilt if something happened."

8. If your partner is constantly complaining about apparently unreal aches and pains and going from doctor to doctor.

9. If your partner continually makes excuses for not finding a job. If he or she borrows money from you frequently. The partner who evades responsibility and who can't manage his money wisely will be a poor marriage risk.

10. If your partner is overly jealous, suspicious, questions your word all the time, feels that everyone is against him.

11. If the one you date is a perfectionist and is constantly critical. This kind of a person often creates a tense unhealthy atmosphere.

12. Treats you contemptuously. Uses biting sarcasm.

13. Parents and other significant people are strongly against your marriage. Consider their reasons before you make a final decision.
14. Lack of spiritual harmony.
15. Few areas of common interest.
16. Inability to accept constructive criticism. Doesn't apologize when he is wrong.

DANGER SIGNS THAT WOULD INDICATE THE NEED FOR PROFESSIONAL COUNSELING

1. Undue jealousy, suspicion, distrust.
2. Constant chip-on-the-shoulder attitude.
3. Temper tantrums.
4. Unresolved anger, resentment. Vindictiveness.
5. Physically abusive.
6. Objects to or is distant to any kind of romantic involvement.
7. Severe mood swings. High elation followed by depression.
8. Constantly negative attitude. Pessimistic.
9. Suspicious of everyone. Suspects some sort of plotting against him.
10. Speaks of suicide and the meaninglessness of life.

ACCEPTANCE

An important quality for each of you to have is a realistic acceptance of that which cannot be changed.

This will include accepting the inevitability of aging with its accompanying deterioration of the body. Although it is probably difficult for you to visualize and accept this now when you are young, you will need to carefully consider the fact that your partner may or may not age gracefully. Inevitably his or her body will begin to be less attractive to you. But if your marriage has been a good one and you and your partner have grown together through the years, your attraction for each other will continue. You need to be aware that in picking a marriage partner it is important to find one who has the potential to grow more attractive with the years as far as personality is concerned. Consistent fellowship with God helps bring this about.

GIVE GOD AN OPTION

Do not unite yourselves with unbelievers; they are no fit mates for you . . . .

2 Corinthians 6:14 NEB

This verse is quoted over and over to young people, especially when Christian parents are concerned that their sons or daughters may be developing a serious relationship with unbelievers. On the other hand, many young people feel that their options for dating seriously, with the possibility of marriage in view, are severely limited. This is especially true of girls, who usually outnumber the boys in any church group. It is possible that the one you will marry may not yet be a believer.

I believe that the young adult, however, should be involved in witnessing to his peers because:

1. Our Lord commands it.
2. Your generation will have a tremendous impact on the cultural climate of our country as your parents' generation ages.
3. You may find your mate among the people whom you lead to Christ. I know of many couples where one was led to Christ by the other *before* marriage. *Don't* count on this happening after marriage.

MARRIAGE COUNSELORS

Fees for marriage counseling may vary anywhere from $25 to $60 a session with $35 as perhaps the average fee. You can expect to see the counselor once or twice a week initially, depending upon the severity of your problem and your willingness to cooperate.

Be wary of a counselor who promises to solve all your problems, who seems to be inordinately interested in your sex life, who advertises flamboyantly, and who is evasive about his qualifications. To date, five states require licensing for marriage counselors. They are California, Michigan, Nevada, New Jersey, and Utah.

REFERRAL SERVICES

Ask your pastor, lawyer, physician, or some other trusted person. These three organizations have a list of Christian counselors throughout the country.

1. Association of Christian Marriage Counselors
   5051 North Central Park Avenue
   Chicago, Illinois 60625
2. Christian Association for Psychological Studies
   6850 Division Avenue, South
   Grand Rapids, Michigan 49508
3. Organization of Christian Counseling Centers
   and Counselors
   342 Madison Avenue
   New York, New York 10017

These two national organizations have a list of professional marriage counselors of varying backgrounds and religious beliefs. You might also look in the Yellow Pages under Marriage and Family Counselors.

1. American Association of Marriage and Family
   Counselors (AAMFC)
   225 Yale Avenue
   Claremont, California 91711
2. The National Alliance for Family Life, Inc.
   (NAFL, Inc.)
   10727 Paramount Boulevard
   Downey, California 90241

QUESTIONS FOR DISCUSSION

1. Why does a person need a philosophy of life and how can it affect his marital happiness?

2. What qualities would you like in a mate and how would they complement your own?

3. Although no one is perfect, what traits would make you cautious about committing yourself to a person in marriage?

Part 2

MAKING THE MOST OF YOUR MARRIAGE

6

So Now You're Engaged

HERE COMES THE BRIDE

It's an awesome moment. There's an air of antici-
pation as the guests wait for the wedding to begin.
From a door near the altar the clergyman emerges,
followed by the groom and his attendants. A sudden
hush . . . and then the organ thunders with the first
notes of the wedding march. The guests rise and half
turn towards the rear of the church to get a glimpse of
the bride as she waits on the arm of her father. The
bridesmaids begin their walk down the aisle. The
groom stands at the altar. This couple have known each
other for years. They dated for a few months and
they've been engaged for a year. And they both know,
at that moment, that they are making an awful mistake.

They knew each other from church. They attended
some youth activities together. Their parents were
friends. When they discovered that they were both
going to enroll in the state university they promised

to look each other up. Coming from a small town, they were unprepared for the impersonal atmosphere of a large university with a student body ten times the size of their town's population. They gravitated to each other out of loneliness and the need for a sense of belonging. Under these circumstances what had been a casual friendship suddenly developed into a powerful infatuation. They announced their engagement at Christmas. By spring vacation their relationship included frequent sexual intercourse. During the summer their attraction for each other had cooled but he felt he had no alternative but to go ahead and marry her because he felt guilty for having promoted their relationship sexually. She felt that she had violated her personal code of ethics and that having "become one" with this man, no other man would marry her. The lines of communication had never been open between them. Each had been a very private person. And so they went through with a marriage that brought nothing but heartache to both of them and severe personality disturbances to their children.

Could this happen to you? At this point in your life you may say a very convincing *no*. But this young couple would have said that it was unthinkable, too, if you had questioned them during their senior year in high school.

To go through with a marriage when you do not feel that you want to share the rest of your life with your partner is not only a stupid mistake, it is an irresponsible act. To put an aura of noble self-sacrifice around the situation is fooling yourself. To saddle another person with a spouse who doesn't love him is cruel. And to bring children into such a relationship is criminal. If you feel, during the engagement, that you don't want to go through with the marriage—don't! Discuss your feelings with your pastor or a professional counselor.

ONE

The concept of *oneness* in marriage necessitates that both partners be willing to compromise when important issues are at stake and when they have differing opinions about a course of action. Learning to give and take is an important step in the building of a sound marriage. And the best time for learning this art is the courtship and engagement period. Statistics show that six months seems to be the most satisfactory length of engagement. Many of those who are divorced have been engaged less than three months. The proportion of those couples actively engaged in sex before marriage rises sharply after eight months.

PRE-ENGAGEMENT COUNSELING

Before you're engaged let me suggest that you have some counseling individually and together. If you are already engaged it is doubly important. This will give you a chance to uncover some of your negative personality traits and hidden deficiencies. Then you will be able to modify and, hopefully, correct some of them before you are committed to a marriage partner and a wedding date. And if, before the date is set, you have some reservations about going through with the marriage, you will be free to resolve them without fear of "what people will say." Many young couples are pressured by families and friends into marriages they are not yet ready for. If you two are the last single couple in a group of close friends who have dated together for a while, you may feel left out if you don't set a date. Girls, especially, are influenced by participating in the prewedding arrangements of their friends. Attending showers for the bride, buying bridesmaids' dresses, being in on the plans for the ceremony and reception — all of these things surround the event with excitement and romanticism. This is the time to remember that maturity means using your head as well as your heart.

LIVING UP TO EXPECTATIONS

As you both think seriously about this marriage that is in your near future, it is helpful to acknowledge that you are living in a highly mobile society. The typical nuclear family that you will become (husband, wife, and children) is under tremendous pressure. The husband and wife are expected to be all things to all people.

The man is expected to be a good provider, a wise money handler, an understanding father, and loving husband. He is also expected to be a model citizen, an active churchman, and a superior performer in his chosen occupation; a considerate son to his parents, a humanitarian, a Christian who teaches by example as well as verbally; a carpenter, plumber, toy repairer, and general Mr. Fix-It; a gardener, banker, comforter to crying children, and able storyteller. And that's just for starters.

And what of his wife? She's supposed to be as beautiful as a model and as comfortable to be with as the girl next door. She's expected to know all about budgets, babies, and balanced meals; car pools, cub scouts, and corporation politics. She's encouraged to improve her mind and combine children and a career if she wants to. She's an amateur psychologist, a husband's best friend, a nurse, a cook, a hostess, and a success in the bedroom. A Sunday-school teacher, a taxi driver, and a woman who doesn't show her age. Sounds pretty imposing, doesn't it?

Now in order to fill all these roles reasonably well you will be involved in constant role changing like a chameleon, on a day-to-day and even hour-to-hour basis. And to make the grade even moderately well you both should be more alike than you are different. One theory holds that some opposites marry because they seem to complement their own weak points by finding a mate who has strength in that area. Many of these marriages are rated as happy, but further study yields the information that the areas where their personality traits are different are usually peripheral ones, and the couple are basically very much alike in the areas where basic conflicts might occur.

You may not have been aware of these factors before your engagement, but it is important that you be aware of them now. You will need to be able to distinguish between the little differences that may come up between you and be resolved by intelligent compromise, and basic personality conflicts that can be resolved only by one partner consistently giving in. This kind of "solution" to conflict can cause growing resentment in the submissive partner, and could ultimately destroy your marriage.

BE REALISTIC

It's important to realize that the honeymoon glow will not last forever. Your reactions to the reality that the one you married is not perfect will depend upon your maturity. When you begin to realize that the person you have married is a real human being, with weaknesses as well as strengths—that's where the test of your maturity begins. The girl who was even-tempered and fun to be with has an occasional grouchy morning. The fellow who was so considerate and thoughtful forgets her birthday. If you are prepared in advance for the inevitable revelation of your partner as a normal human being rather than the embodiment of perfection, you won't be so disturbed when this occurs. The sign of a mature love is the ability of the partners to love each other unconditionally, in spite of faults. There is nothing more threatening to a marriage or to the relationship between a parent and child, than to realize that love is given for good behavior and withdrawn for poor behavior. The relationship then involves a constant seesaw of emotional giving and withholding, and results in constant feelings of insecurity. When the partner is being loved he is wondering how long before he will be unloved. How fortunate we are that God does not treat us in this way. We are always loved, even though our behavior is not always approved of.

And we can see that it was while we were powerless to help ourselves that Christ died for sinful men. In human experience it is a rare thing for one man to give his life for another, even if the latter be a good man, though there have been a few who have had the courage to do it. Yet the proof of God's amazing love is this: that it was *while we were sinners* that Christ died for us.

Romans 5:6–8 PHILLIPS

VISITS

I hope that you and your partner have had opportunities to visit in each other's homes before your engagement. This is the time to see your intended mate in his or her home surroundings and within the family circle. Couples need to be aware that there are three families involved in this new relationship of marriage. First, the family you have come out of. Next, the family you will be marrying into, your in-laws. Third, the new family unit you will be establishing. You will need to give some thought to the personalities of your future mate's parents and the kind of home they have established. This is because many of the parents' traits will be imbedded in your mate and he or she may be inclined to perpetuate the kind of home that has become familiar.

For example, in a home where the future wife's father is dominant, her concept of marriage is one where the husband is the head of the house. If the man she is marrying is a weak person, who does not assert himself and lacks self-confidence, both of them could be unhappy. Or perhaps you come from a home where everything is neat and in place most of the time. When you visit your future mate's home you may be surprised to find that everything looks like a mess. That family is comfortable living like that and it will be hard to change your intended mate's personal habits. You may decide, instead, to be prepared to endure sloppiness because of the many good qualities he or she has. You may decide to be the partner who will do the picking up now and then to make the home look better. Or you may feel that, given the opportunity and some encouragement, the other person may make a real effort to please you by learning to be neater. However, don't marry with the idea that you're going to change your mate.

It is also helpful to study carefully the parents of your future mate and how they behave towards each other and towards their children. Parents who are not meeting each other's needs emotionally often develop an abnormal interest in the lives of their children and this interest may take the form of prying and dominating even after you are married.

HIDDEN DANGER

Many couples do not realize that as individuals they are products not only of their family relationships but of all of their interpersonal relationships plus their own will. It is important for the couple to discover any buried feelings that may not have surfaced during the dating period. Often couples wear masks, figuratively speaking, during their courtship. These masks should be relinquished during the engagement period. Such feelings of resentment, hostility, and inferiority can rob the marital relationship of a great deal of happiness, especially if they are compounded by an inability to love or show affection.

Sometimes couples don't realize that there is a strong competitive spirit between them and so they enter marriage with a severe handicap. They may be tempted to bolster their own ego by cutting the other one down. When people like this marry, their relationship becomes soured when they realize that they are doomed to continue years of quarreling because they are each trying to beat the other in some way, rather than becoming teammates and pulling for the same goals.

All of these things should be discovered and discussed before marriage. The significance of premarriage counseling as opposed to postmarriage counseling is that you have time to work at becoming a more emotionally healthy person before you marry. In the physical realm, preventing a disease is always preferable to curing it, and in the emotional realm the same analogy applies to counseling. One of the most satisfying aspects of my work is to introduce people's real selves to themselves.

YOUR FUTURE

It is also important in premarriage counseling for me to find out to what extent the couple have discussed housing, finances, and family planning. Will the wife continue to work after marriage and, if so, how does the man feel about this? What are their mutual interests, their hobbies, their level of education, their attitudes toward sex, toward authority? How do they feel about each other's friends and relatives? Do I detect the possibility of a power struggle between them? If they are Christians, to what extent are they committed to Christ? Are they concerned about being controlled by the Holy Spirit? Or is one content to be merely a churchgoer? As a couple are they praying seriously about their coming marriage?

SPIRITUAL ATTITUDES

Meeting each other's needs on a spiritual level and learning to grow together in your Christian faith are vital aspects of marriage for the Christian. If you find that your intended mate shies away from the idea of visiting a professional marriage counselor, suggest a visit to your clergyman. After this he may feel more

comfortable about following your suggestion for professional counseling.

Sometimes an engaged couple will come for counseling and I will find that one is a Christian and the
other is a nonbeliever. The Christian is usually aware
that the Bible is very definite about not being unequally yoked together. But he will usually justify
marriage with this kind of rationalizing: "I have never
met anyone like him before. The Christians I've dated
are dull. We are very compatible and very much in love.
Surely God would rather have me marry this person
than someone who is a believer but whom I don't love."

There are several flaws in this reasoning.

1. A committed Christian's first obligation is to be
   in the will of God and this presupposes obedience
   to the Word of God.
2. A Christian's source of power to perform in any
   situation is the Holy Spirit who lives in him. His
   source of guidance is this same Holy Spirit. His
   link with this power is through prayer. The biblical principle intending to restrict the marriage
   option of Christians to other Christians is for our
   benefit. Two Christians, indwelt by the Holy
   Spirit, subject to His guidance, open to His power,
   and exercising the privilege of prayer, have a
   tremendous thing going for them in building a
   happy, fulfilling, long-lasting marriage that will
   result in blessing each other.
3. By contrast, the unequally yoked couples' re-

sources are not only halved, but the Christian's effectiveness as a believer is diminished to the extent that he, in an effort to maintain marital harmony, agrees to decisions that are not motivated by the Holy Spirit.

4. The Christian is presupposing that God isn't able to guide him to a suitable marriage partner who will be a Christian.

Sometimes the Christian partner will tell me that she is convinced that her fiancé will become a believer after they marry. Perhaps, but probably not. Occasionally an unbeliever will profess to have accepted Christ as Saviour, but if there is no evidence of any change at all during the engagement period this should serve as a warning sign not to go ahead. Some Christians are disappointed after marriage to find that one who claimed to have become a believer during the courtship apparently did so just to please the other and assure that the marriage would take place, but there was no serious intent behind the supposed commitment. That is why it is wise to see that such a person gives evidence of his sincere desire to follow the Lord before the wedding.

For the Christian couple there is an additional area where potential problems may go unrecognized. If one of them has a relationship with Christ that has prompted a decision to put the will of God first in his life and the extent of the other's spiritual growth is to go to church on Sundays and live with self-will uppermost, then the stage is set for alienation between them. What each of them does as a spouse, a parent, an employee, a citizen, may be based on entirely different concepts. How they spend their money, where they go for entertainment, the kinds of friends they select, the type of church they attend, the pattern of family worship—or lack of it— all of these areas are potential trouble spots for such a couple. During this time of getting to know each other better such questions need to be fully and frankly discussed.

LAST CHANCE!

If you haven't asked yourself the following questions prior to your engagement, the engagement period is your last chance to ask them.

1. Why am I going to get married to this person?
2. If this person had no sexual appeal to me, would I still feel that he or she would make a good friend whose companionship I would enjoy and whose conversation wouldn't bore me?
3. Will this person make a good parent for my children?

If you are getting married because you are lonely, bored, afraid, frustrated, pregnant, or embarrassed to be the unmarried one among your friends, then it would be wise for you to give some serious thought to whether you should continue the engagement. The only valid reason for anyone to get married is "because I believe God wants me to spend the rest of my life with this person whom I love and respect and these are his reasons also." This means exactly what it says—the rest of your life. Not "till misunderstandings do us part," or until he or she loses physical attractiveness, or until I find someone better, or until I'm tired of responsibility and decide to enjoy my freedom.

QUESTIONS FOR DISCUSSION

1. How can a couple who are really serious with each other use their courtship and engagement period to ensure a happier marriage relationship?
2. Under what conditions should a person break an engagement?
3. Why do you think the Lord forbids Christians from marrying nonbelievers, even though they may be nice people?

7

Cutting Loose

IT'S DIFFICULT

Many Christians are torn internally because on the one hand they feel God is calling them in one direction, but their parents are pulling them in another direction. Some parents play the guilt game, reminding their children how they sacrificed for them and took care of them. It is not my intention to minimize the sacrifices of mothers and fathers for their children. Many parents do deprive themselves of the necessities of life. Many have worked for years at underpaid, backbreaking jobs to get a son or daughter through college. Some have lived in unheated apartments, without sufficient food or clothes. But the parents who suffered are the ones who should say, "I'm grateful to God for his provision." When Christian parents sacrifice for their children, they should be doing this "as unto the Lord."

Parents should give out of love and a desire to

help, not with strings attached. But if they expect pay-
ment in terms of obedience; if they use their gifts to
insure that they will continue to be the decision-
makers in their children's lives, then the help can be
classed as a bribe, harsh as that may sound. The trag-
edy is that for years after a parent has put a son or
daughter through college and the grown child is married, working, and raising a family, the parents often
expect the "repayment" to be continued, not necessarily in money, but by:

1. Having a part in decision-making.
2. Expecting the couple and their family to visit
   frequently.
3. Criticizing.
4. Continuing to play the part of the parent as dominant with the grown child as submissive.

A sensitive adult child, realizing that the financial
help given to him by his parents has made a significant contribution to getting him where he is, gives in
because he would feel guilty or ungrateful if he didn't.

The commandment to honor thy father and mother
does not mean that the parent has a right to be in control of that child all of his life. All this does is provoke
the children to anger. Certainly the resentment and
hatred that may result do not honor them! Many parents will never experience the joy of having their children become their friends because they don't treat
them as adults. These same parents are actually the
architects of their own loneliness and unhappiness

because they want closeness from their children whom they won't accept as adult friends. Unwittingly they push their children away. What adult child wants to visit his parents, knowing that they will be criticized for the way they dress, budget their money, vote, or bring up their children?

GOD'S WORD

When young people are faced with problems involving their own parents or their intended spouse's parents, the most helpful suggestion I can give them is one that can be offered for any problem. Before you take any other problem-solving action, ask God to show you what biblical principle *you* may be violating in the situation. In the case of interfering parents I usually find that the young couple has not put into practice the verse:

> For this reason a man shall leave his father and his mother and shall be joined to his wife, and the two shall become one flesh.
>
> Ephesians 5:31 AMPLIFIED

This process of leaving one's parents should begin to take place long before a son or daughter marries. To leave them implies being emotionally and economically independent of them. While you do this on the physical level after marriage, moving out of your parental home and into a new home, on the emotional level this process of leaving doesn't take place automatically and simultaneously. Gradually a young person has to learn to make his own decisions, be responsible for his own behavior and the results of that behavior, adopt a set of standards or ethics that are truly his own—and not simply those he has inherited from his parents, accepted from his church, or acquired from his peers. This sort of independence or leaving is a normal and necessary part of maturing. If leaving doesn't take place prior to your engagement period, then you can expect many problems, not only between you and your parents, but between you and the person you have chosen to marry.

This biblical admonition to leave his father and his mother first appears in the Genesis record of man's creation, and enunciates a basic psychological principle —that emotional maturity, as indicated by a healthy independence from one's parents, is necessary for a happy marriage. The more emotionally dependent on parents a marriage partner is, the less chance there is for happiness in that marriage.

CHRISTIAN RESPONSIBILITY

What we've said so far about this subject applies whether the participants are Christians or nonbelievers. But there is an added responsibility in the spiritual sense for those who have committed their lives to Christ.

If God instructs us to leave father and mother emotionally by the time we marry and if we are reluctant to be our own man or our own woman because our parents will raise a fuss, then in effect we are saying that the price of obeying Christ's instructions comes too high. We would rather have peace at any price. If this is the conclusion that you may have reached then perhaps it would be helpful to remind you that by your lack of positive action to cut loose from domineering parents, you are indicating that their love and approval means more to you than your love for your mate, which is a violation of Ephesians 5:31.

"But, Dr. Florio," you may say, "you just don't know how difficult my parents [or in-laws] can be!" From listening to hundreds of young couples, I can assure you that I do know. But I can also tell you that your parents' attitudes and behavior are not likely to improve with age. The time to set the pattern for your future relationship with them is *now*, and once the repercussions die down and they realize that you and your future mate are serious about obeying Christ, putting Him first in your individual lives and in your new corporate life as a married couple, they may surprise you with their reasonableness.

MOTIVATIONS

Parents, as a rule, don't spend their spare time thinking up ways to meddle in your affairs. Quite likely their motivation for such meddling is hidden even from themselves. Often the marriage of a son or daughter takes place when their other children are away at college or living independently. Suddenly the parents, especially the mother, may be aware for the first time that they are not needed as they once were.

Also, someone else has come into their child's life to take first place. Both parents may be victims of a preoccupation with the negative aspects of aging. There is something about a fiftieth birthday that signals depression to some individuals. Perhaps the parents are undergoing a period of stress and reevaluation of goals in their own marriage. All of these "perhaps" situations are tension-producing and may cause parents to become overinvolved in their children's lives. However, this doesn't excuse you from exercising your obligation to cut loose from your emotional dependence on them.

ALL THINGS—FOR GOOD

If you have problem parents, thank God as the Bible says: "In every thing give thanks: for this is the will of God in Christ Jesus concerning you" (1 Thessalonians 5:18), for the opportunity you have to experience some important lessons. For the opportunity to increase your faith, trust, and dependency on Christ. For the opportunity to demonstrate love towards an "enemy." I feel it is possible to have love for a person like this without necessarily respecting or liking them. Jesus had love for the Pharisees who were planning to put Him to death, but He didn't respect or like them the way He did Lazarus his friend, when He went to his graveside and wept.

We may not be able to do as perfect a job as Jesus Christ did, but the key to keeping the roots of bitterness from growing is to focus on our relationship to our Lord.

> Thou wilt keep him in perfect peace, whose mind
> is stayed on thee; because he trusteth in thee.
>
> Isaiah 26:3

When we focus on Jesus Christ we can consciously reject from our minds negative, debilitating thoughts.

We might compare our preoccupation with negative thoughts to the process of digging a deep trench. Into this ditch is poured thoughts of resentment, revenge, hatred, self-pity, vindictiveness. A person realizes that it took him a long time to dig this trench, filled with foul-smelling garbage. It won't be easy to pile enough dirt on it to cover it completely. But as he makes a diligent effort, putting one shovelful of Spirit-motivated love and patience into the trench at regular intervals, someday he will fill in that garbage dump. When he will accept the fact that he has fallen into the pit of resentment, he can decide to climb out of it, by a gradual process, rather than staying in that pit and wallowing around in hatred and self-pity.

There is a practical prayer you can use to help yourself with this problem, and the same technique will help you with other problems, also. You will want to change some of the wording to suit your circumstances and thought style.

> I know what I'm doing.
> I've allowed myself to slip into
> the garbage pit again, Lord,
> and I've even enjoyed wallowing
> around in all that self-pity.

God, help me climb out.
Satan wants me to stay.

I'm sorry for wasting the time and energy
I should be using to serve You
and to be relating to those I love.

When I think of Your sacrifice on the cross
to save me,
When I think of all You have in store for me
in eternity,
There is no excuse for me to waste time
Wallowing around in garbage.

Make a habit of repeating this whenever you fall
into that pit. In a desperate moment when you can't
even exercise the will to repeat this prayer, call out to
God, "Jesus, help me out!" And you'll find help. This
is the power available to those who commit themselves to Jesus Christ. Now there are some people who
just sink farther and farther down into depression and
anger and perhaps even behave irrationally. When I
counsel with them I find that the reason for their
powerlessness is that they haven't taken the first step
before they pray. They have blamed everybody but
themselves for their predicament! It isn't what people
say to us that harms us the most, it is how we react to
their words that does the harm. With God's help you can
control your reactions if you really want to, but most
of us prefer to focus on pitying ourselves.

HANDLING ANGER

Somebody is going to say, "Does all this mean that I must never feel angry and if I do I ought to feel guilty?" No! Don't feel guilty because a parent, peer, or partner provoked you to anger. Say to yourself something like this:

I have been provoked to anger and I feel angry.

It's all right for me to feel angry.

God allows me to feel anger.

It is not natural to be provoked and then squelch those angry feelings.

Jesus didn't squelch his anger in the temple and Paul became angry with the church at Corinth.

So it's all right to feel angry.

If I squelch my legitimate anger, I can become ill, and depressed.

But I must not allow these angry feelings to fester and become feelings of bitterness, hatred, and self-pity.

If I allow *that* to happen then I *ought* to feel guilty and confess my guilt to God.

So when I'm provoked to anger I will pray, and I'll go for a walk, cut the grass, go for a swim, chop some wood, scrub the floor, play ball, saw some wood, or hammer some nails.

This will relieve my tensions and deflate my anger and when it is gone I'll be at peace with myself, and with my enemy, and with God.

And when you pray it might go something like this:

Lord Jesus Christ, I'm so glad that You have experienced these same problems so You know how I feel.

Keep me from overreacting to having been hurt or treated this way.

Help me to react the way You would want me to.

Keep me from retaliating.

I'll have to turn this other individual over into Your hands.

Lord Jesus, I thank You that I have an understanding friend like You who can understand how I feel.

Help me to cope with this situation whether it is changed or remains unchanged.

Your greatest test will come when you are called on to walk the extra mile, to turn your other cheek, to love your enemy. This requires supernatural assistance. This supernatural power is available to you through the Holy Spirit living in you. Draw on His power—experience it—and paradoxically, it will help you to grow.

QUESTIONS FOR DISCUSSION

1. Why isn't the commandment to honor your father and mother inconsistent with the Lord's words, "He who loves father and mother more than me is not worthy of me"?
2. What conditions might make it hard for an adult child to let go of his parents or for his parents to let go of him?
3. How can a preoccupation with negative thoughts affect one's personal and marital happiness?
4. How do you eliminate negative thoughts?

8

Sex: Will It Make or Break Your Marriage?

LEARN TO LOVE WISELY

A lot of Christians are unhappily married because their basic sex needs are not being met. Some are getting divorced while others are maintaining their marriages but having affairs. Don't keep the lid on your sexual feelings before marriage to such an extent that it will take the rest of your life to get it off. Value your virginity but don't repress every thought and expression of love to the extent that you need professional therapy after marriage to help you release the pent-up emotions that have been dammed because of unhealthy attitudes.

Certain young people find themselves in trouble in spite of their religious upbringing, not because their sex drives propel them into immoral behavior, but because they are propelled into immoral behavior by overreacting to feeling unloved, unwanted, and misunderstood.

A good sexual relationship doesn't come about automatically. Ideally, you receive a sound sexual education and the proper respect for sex from your parents; you put it into practice after marriage. The church should reinforce what has been taught at home. However, many young people are involved in premarital sex now. With some couples the reason for a sexual relationship before marriage has been heavy petting that got out of control. A number of girls that I have talked to at a home for unwed mothers said that they had no intention of having intercourse, but "one thing led to another and here I am." This is like the child who stood at the edge of a forest fire and said, "But I only lit a match."

Other couples succumb to the notion that "we're as good as married anyway in God's sight, so why not complete the marriage? Why wait until the wedding and a few words by the preacher?" Many such couples change their minds about marrying and break the engagement. In some individuals the guilt feelings become barriers to adjusting to marriage with another partner. I have had to counsel women who were unable to be sexually responsive to their husbands and the husbands of such women who became impotent because of constant rejection. And, in many instances, the problems stemmed from guilt.

A question that often leads young couples into premarital sex is this one: "How do you know if you and your intended mate will be sexually compatible without intercourse before marriage?" There is nothing wrong with a young couple starting their marriage inexperienced in sex. But there is a difference between being inexperienced and being ignorant and unwilling to learn. Such ignorance and unwillingness can ruin your marriage. If your attitude has been healthy and wholesome because of positive conditioning from your parents, then you are fortunate. But you can still benefit from reading and discussion. Two books you might want to consider are *Sexual Understanding Before Marriage* and *Sexual Happiness in Marriage*, both by Herbert J. Miles.

SERIOUS COMPLICATIONS

One of the greatest insults a girl can receive before marriage is the "proposition." "If you really love me, prove it." Her reply ought to be, "If you really love me, you wouldn't ask me to prove it in a way that would violate my standards." One of the greatest compliments a girl can receive is, "Let me spend the rest of my life with you."

CASE HISTORY

Jerry and Ellen came to me after being married seven years. Jerry was hostile and bitter towards his wife. "She must have been a great little actress, all right," he said. "She seemed like everything I ever wanted in a wife. She was good-natured, loving, and fun to be with. After the preacher pronounced us man and wife she froze up and treated me like I was a leper.

She gets mad at me for every little thing. She says things that hurt and sometimes she seems to enjoy doing it. Ellen's always too tired or she's got a headache or something when I want to make love to her."

After some sessions with Ellen, I discovered what had caused her abrupt change in behavior. The night before their wedding Jerry had persuaded her to have intercourse with him. "After all, we're as good as married," he had told her. When she hesitated, he became annoyed and accused her of not really loving him.

As Ellen sat in my office, she continued her story. "I finally gave in because I didn't want to hurt him. So we went into the back seat of the car. He was in a hurry because the cops patrol that area. It wasn't at all the way I had pictured it would be. The next day when I walked down that aisle in my grandmother's white wedding gown I was heartbroken. I had always pictured myself walking down that aisle and symbolically giving myself to Jerry and afterwards when we would be alone, when he would really make me his wife, I thought it would be . . . well . . . this might seem silly . . . but sort of a holy feeling about our being one, like the Bible says. I was so disappointed that it couldn't be that way. Frankly, Dr. Florio, the night before just wasn't worth it." Then I asked her if that could be why she treated Jerry so mean? "I don't really know . . . I've never analyzed it. But I guess it's because I do blame him for spoiling the beginning of our marriage. I had wanted to stay a virgin until I got married and I don't seem to be able to forgive Jerry for taking that from me."

When Jerry realized how Ellen felt he was surprised and chagrined. It had never occurred to him that girls could prize their virginity so much. Or that they could feel guilty and resentful about losing it before being married.

When Jerry asked Ellen to forgive him for being so thoughtless and selfish, she did, but it wasn't easy for her and it took some time. In the months that followed Jerry tried to show patience and understanding when she reverted to her old pattern. These young people are working hard to salvage their marriage. They were wise to get help. They would have been wiser to have gotten help when the trouble first started, and of course the whole problem could have been avoided if they hadn't violated the biblical command on premarital chastity.

HEALTHY ATTITUDES

One of the important goals in marriage ought to be for the husband and wife to become masterful lovers. Our basic hunger for sexual fulfillment is given by God. Christ Himself compared His relationship to His church to the relationship of bridegroom to his bride.

You are a sexual being and acceptance of that fact is necessary to good mental health. You need to acknowledge the fact that you have sexual organs and sexual feelings. You need to accept your sexuality as a gift from God. To satisfy this drive is natural and right. God established the marriage relationship so that this drive could be satisfied not only on the physical level, but in loving commitment to and communion with one's mate. Man's thoughts and emotions are imprisoned unless they are expressed through the vehicle of his body, and so in marriage both the husband and the wife express their love for each other in the union of their bodies. This was the design for man's basic interpersonal unit and the foundation on which the family was to be built. Before you and your prospective mate marry, it is vitally important that each of you have, or develop, a healthy attitude towards your own sexuality, and toward intercourse in your marriage. It is necessary to eliminate the attitude of past generations that sex was dirty, disgusting, a hush-hush subject, and something that a woman had to endure. If there is any trace of an attitude like this in your thinking, you should get help in changing your thinking before you marry. Sometimes a person who has been raised in a Christian home picks up the idea that spirituality and sex are incompatible. We were not created as disembodied spirits and it is not a mark of Christian maturity that a man or woman feels "too spiritual" to enjoy a normal sexual relationship in marriage.

A lukewarm attitude towards sex is sometimes manifested by the mother-dominated man who has grown up with a weak image of his own masculinity. Unless he is helped to understand this before marriage, he may begin to suffer psychological trauma and anxiety when he begins to seriously doubt his own masculinity because of his inadequate performance as a husband.

SECRETS

Should you both "tell all" before the wedding? This is a question that is frequently asked of the pastor or counselor and one which can't be answered by a simple yes or no. If you have ever taken drugs, been institutionalized, been married before, had children without the benefit of marriage, are in debt, have had venereal disease, you should give complete information to your future mate. In the matter of previous sexual experience it is better to confess it but let the matter end there. It is probably best not to give names, dates, or details. These would tend to fix the episode more firmly in the partner's mind and would probably serve no useful purpose. The main reasons for being honest with each other in this respect is to prevent a feeling of guilt over something that must be kept secret from one's mate and to protect the mate from finding out from some other source. People in love and with emotional maturity are usually willing to understand and forgive. If they can't, then you shouldn't marry them because they will throw it up to you for the rest of your life. The biblical principle of forgiving others because Christ has forgiven you is dramatically illustrated in the parable of the king who forgave his servant a large debt.

For the kingdom of Heaven is like a king who decided to settle his accounts with his servants.

When he had started calling in his accounts, a man was brought to him who owed him millions of dollars. And when it was plain that he had no means of repaying the debt, his master gave orders for him to be sold as a slave, and his wife and children and all his possessions as well, and the money to be paid over. At this the servant fell on his knees before his master, "Oh, be patient with me!" he cried, "and I will pay you back every penny!" Then his master was moved with pity for him, set him free and canceled the debt.

But when this same servant had left his master's presence, he found one of his fellow servants who owed him a few dollars. He grabbed him and seized him by the throat, crying, "Pay up what you owe me!" At this his fellow servant fell down at his feet, and implored him, "Oh, be patient with me, and I will pay you back!" But he refused and went out and had him put in prison until he should repay the debt.

When the other fellow servants saw what had happened, they were horrified and went and told their master the whole incident. Then his master called him in. "You wicked servant!" he said, "Didn't I cancel all that debt when you begged me to do so? Oughtn't you to have taken pity on your fellow servant as I, your master, took pity on you?" And his master in anger handed him over to the

jailers till he should repay the whole debt. This is
how my Heavenly Father will treat you unless you
forgive your brother from your heart.

Matthew 18:23–35 PHILLIPS

WORRIES

What about the person who has experienced feelings of sexual attraction towards a member of his or
her own sex? Does this mean that they will have problems in adjusting to the heterosexual relationship in
marriage? Many such young people worry themselves
into a tense state about this sort of thing, when all
they had experienced was a natural phase in the process of growing up. In the normal course of events a
child's focus of love is on a member of the opposite
sex. But then there is a period during which members
of one's own sex become the focus of affection. At
varying ages, depending on many factors, the young
person begins to find members of the opposite sex
particularly attractive. In most instances the average
adolescent transfers his interest to a heterosexual relationship. Those who are unable to do so, or who find
that both sexes attract them equally, should have
competent professional counseling before any definite
plans are made for marriage. Even the practicing homo-
sexuals or lesbians can be helped if their motivation is
strong enough. Some of you may have such a problem
but hesitate to look for help because it would embarrass
you to admit to these feelings. But without help before
marriage, you may find that your relationship with

your mate will be damaged and this will affect his emotional well-being and yours, and possibly warp the emotional development of any children you may have.

Don and Marcy had already announced their engagement when they came to me for counseling. They had heard that it was the thing to do before marriage but they didn't feel that they had any serious problems or any conspicuous personality flaws.

When I interviewed Marcy and asked if she was happy during this engagement period, she answered yes immediately, but then looked thoughtful for a moment as though she might have some reservations. After further questioning I discovered that Don hadn't been demonstrative to her while they were dating. She expected that after their engagement was announced, he would put his arms around her occasionally, especially when they were alone. She expected more than a peck on the cheek when he kissed her goodnight after a date. And she didn't see anything wrong with holding hands. "Sometimes I find myself feeling disappointed," she said, "but then I realize that Don's parents are Christians and brought him up to be a real gentleman who really respects a woman. So I guess I shouldn't let it bother me."

"Have you discussed this with him?" I asked.

"No," she said. "Our being married will make a difference."

Suppose Marcy was right. Suppose Don's parents had taught him to repress the showing of affection before marriage on the assumption that any bodily contact would lead to a forbidden intimacy. If so, then Don needed aid in developing a healthy yet moral attitude towards love and its physical expression. But Marcy was wrong in her diagnosis. The problem turned out to be a harder one to resolve. When I talked with Don he readily admitted that he found it difficult to express affection towards any girl, and it had always been this way since he started dating. Don wanted to marry Marcy; he felt that he loved her. But he couldn't bring himself to think about intercourse and in his thinking any physical expressions of affection were almost in the same category.

It was obvious that Don had a serious personality disturbance and I urged them to delay setting a date for the wedding until his problem had been substantially resolved.

As we proceeded with further appointments it developed that Don's father had been an absentee parent for most of his son's formative years. His father had traveled extensively and was home only on weekends. Consequently, Don's mother had, of necessity, assumed the dominant role in the home, and her son had identified with her rather than the male image of his father. Her frequent belittling of Don compounded the problem. As a result he had been crippled emotionally. Although there had never been any overt involvement in a homosexual relationship, as a Christian Don was troubled with guilt feelings because of a slight attraction to men. In an effort to cover up his feelings, he had chosen to marry Marcy, the only girl he felt he could be happy with as a lifetime companion. But sex hadn't entered into the picture at all and he was dreading the sexual intimacy of marriage.

I wish I could tell you that Don and Marcy finally got married and that they are living happily ever after. But such isn't the case. Both young people realized that Don's hang-up was a very real obstacle to a happy marriage. Don is being treated on an intensive basis and Marcy is patiently waiting. When friends ask when they are going to set the date their answer is a good one for any couple intending to marry. "We'll set the date just as soon as we feel that we are ready for all the responsibilities of marriage."

Marcy made three serious mistakes.

1. In trying to assign a reason for Don's odd behavior she came up with the wrong answer.
2. She put off discussing the problem with him.
3. She neglected to get premarital counseling before the engagement was announced. The delay was costly in terms of the longer treatment involved and the deferred marriage.

Couples often make plans many months ahead for the kind of furniture they will buy, the apartment or house they will live in, the make of car they will drive. They plan and budget for these expenses. They will spend many hours together planning the wedding trip and making travel arrangements. But they may overlook planning and budgeting for the most important insurance they could have towards developing a happy

and rewarding marriage, premarriage counseling con-
sultations.

QUESTIONS FOR DISCUSSION

1. If God Himself created in us the hunger for sex as
   well as the hunger for food, why does He put conditions on satisfying the sex drive?
2. What steps can a Christian couple take to keep
   their sexual feelings from getting out of control?
3. Why is it essential for a couple to enter marriage
   with healthy attitudes about sex?
4. You have all heard the expression, "If you haven't
   forgotten you haven't forgiven." Is this realistically possible? What factors could help or hinder
   one's ability to forgive and forget?

9

Goals

WHY SET GOALS?

As your marriage day approaches you will be busy with many activities, separately and together. But much of your time will be spent in discussing the practical aspects of the ceremony and wedding trip, and the earlier unhurried pace of your engagement period will be over. It was during this earlier time that you probably talked about the things that were most important to you as persons.

Young people in love discuss their hopes and dreams for the future in glowing terms—and often in nebulous concepts. It's usually, "Someday we'll have a house of our own," or "It would be fun to travel in our future," or "Maybe the Lord will give us some kind of a ministry someday." But these kinds of hopes are sometimes forgotten in the busy years of early marriage, or are replaced by less lofty ones, if disillusionment sets in.

It is helpful for couples in love and planning to marry to come to some kind of agreement as to the goals they will seek together. If not, a husband may find that his dream of having photography for a hobby is taking all the money that his wife has thought she might use to finish her voice studies. Or a wife's dream of having a baby during their second year of marriage is shattered because her husband had figured on her working for three or four years so that they could buy a house of their own.

MISUNDERSTANDINGS

Bob and Dee were caught in that kind of predicament. They had never discussed goals in marriage in any depth—just the usual "let's someday" variety of daydreaming. After they were married Dee discovered that Bob expected her to spend every weekend camping in nearby state parks. She knew that he had gone camping with friends when she first knew him, but he hadn't gone regularly while they were dating. He enjoyed hiking and they used to hike some of the trails on holidays, but she supposed this was a sometime thing that he liked to do occasionally. She couldn't understand it when he insisted that they camp every weekend.

It turned out that Bob had had a boyhood dream of someday being able to go camping whenever he wanted to. He had always had to wait "until you are older" when he was a child, or "if you can get someone else to go with you," when he was in his teens. And often there wasn't enough money for the kind of camping equipment he wanted. Now that he was married, Bob thought that on their combined salaries he could buy the equipment he had always wanted and that he could count on his wife to go with him and enjoy every weekend camping, hiking, fishing, and cooking over an open fire.

They were married in the spring and by fall Dee was looking forward to the winter when she thought it would be too cold to make camp. But by that time Bob had plans to buy a piece of land in ski country and construct a simple A-line chalet so they could go up every weekend and ski. It was then that Dee insisted on a long overdue serious discussion of mutually agreed upon goals for their marriage.

She had no objection to going camping or skiing one weekend a month if Bob would agree to take her to a musical event of some kind one Saturday night a month. Bob was so disappointed at this turn of events that Dee decided she would compromise on two weekends a month camping if he would agree to do something she wanted to do on the other weekends, including staying at home, having some friends in, or working together on refinishing some of their bargain antiques.

It was a hard adjustment for Bob to make, and there was some resentment on his part which made him decide to get counseling. When I talked to them I found that it had never occurred to either of them that a discussion of such goals prior to marriage was imperative!

ADAPTABILITY

Sometimes the goals cause disagreements, but there is one mutually satisfying goal that would help the marriage of every couple, and that is to agree that together you will work at becoming adaptable marriage partners.

This means that each one of you will try to modify some of your likes or dislikes if they interfere with the pleasure or convenience of the other. If Frank hates even the smell of liver cooking and Lynn just loves it once a week, Lynn will have it at lunchtime in the school cafeteria so Frank won't have to smell it cooking. On the other hand, Lynn is used to going to bed with a headful of curlers that make her resemble a science-fiction writer's concept of a Martian. She's always done this since she's been in her teens. But that was when she wasn't married to a man who loved her and wanted to share that love without being turned off by a head full of hardware. So when Lynn found out that it bothered her husband so much, she arranged to have her hair styled so she didn't need more than heated rollers on the ends for a short time. And she did this by getting up a half-hour earlier in the morning and getting breakfast with them in her hair. Her husband was showering and shaving during that time and it didn't bother him at all. Adaptation to a mate's desires helped the marriage.

Hal adapted to his wife's habit of sleeping until noon on Saturday, although it wasn't easy at first. He is an energetic extrovert with lots of pep. He's up at seven even on weekends and seldom seems to tire. So instead of making life miserable for Ann by teasing until she dragged herself out of bed to go to the shore, he has hit on a happy solution. While Ann is sleeping he goes over to the local gym for a morning of tennis and swimming in the pool. He's home at 11:00 and Ann has agreed to get up by then and have brunch ready. By noon they're on their way to the shore. It's a shorter time at the beach than Hal would like, but he has gotten in some swimming at the gym to compensate for it.

There are a number of different ways in which couples can learn to adapt to each other's patterns of behavior and, hopefully, you will be able to work out your own ways. The habits and quirks of our mates aren't all visible before marriage and the necessity of adapting afterward comes as a surprise. But if they have both decided beforehand on a goal of becoming adaptable, the chances of friction are very much lessened. Occasionally I do find couples who have discussed their goals before they married. And sometimes there are still complications after the couple says "I do." This often comes about because one of the partners agreed to a goal that the other partner was enthusiastic about, but after the marriage, failed to live up to the agreement.

MONEY PROBLEMS

This happens frequently when a man or woman is enthusiastic about saving money as a goal. Perhaps he or she comes from a family where thrift was important and it was considered a challenge to find ways to live well on a small income. Bargain hunting was fun and each member of the family took pride in dressing well without spending a lot of money. Before marriage, the engaged couple agree that this will be their pattern and this will help them save money for a future home or some other worthwhile cause. But one of the partners has come from a home where thrift was unimportant — you bought what you wanted or needed and if you were in the red at the end of the month you borrowed to tide you over. This partner had agreed in principle to the idea of a thrift goal, but had no intention of changing his spendthrift ways after marriage. And so there has been a deception. After the wedding this partner had credit cards for every major store in town. He is always going to make up the difference in the budget the following month but somehow never does. Sometimes the couple find themselves on the edge of insolvency and a serious strain is put on the marriage. If you agree to a goal simply out of a desire to avoid an argument, the day of reckoning will come. It would be preferable to be honest about your feelings, even at the price of an argument.

This matter of finances is high on the list of potential problem areas. It has been estimated that over 90 percent of the population have financial worries. It is important before a couple marries to talk over their individual attitudes about money. Who handles it? What kind of priorities for the spending of money will be set? What about life insurance? Does the couple feel that it is important for the wife to continue to work? Or if the husband's ego is weak, does he feel it is more important to forego the added income in order to have his wife stay home? Will the wife feel resentment if she is confined to homemaking? What will they save towards? How do they feel about starting a family?

You can see that if the man and woman have sharp differences of opinion about these matters, it is important for them to be resolved before they become husband and wife. The whole shape of their marriage will be adversely affected if the first few years of their relationship are marred by constant bickering about which one will have his way. If you are engaged, you would be wise to seek competent, professional advice regarding budgeting, insurance, and drawing up wills.

QUESTIONS FOR DISCUSSION

1. What goals should a couple discuss during their engagement that will enhance their marital happiness?
2. What is the difference between a couple setting up a goal and commitment to that goal?
3. What is the difference between compromising, accommodating, or adjusting, and complete submission or subjugation in marriage?

10

Happily Ever After?

The focus of this book has been on marriage and some of its problems and how to deal with them. You have been encouraged to ask yourself some pertinent questions. Are you ready for marriage? And if so, how can you go about insuring maximum happiness in your marriage?

You will need to understand yourself in order to evaluate your assets and your liabilities. When that is done and you can see how you appear to others as well as to yourself, you will have a composite picture of the kind of person you are now. You can get trained counseling to help you understand what influences shaped your negative characteristics and, if you are motivated to change them, to help you do that, also. These same aids to self-understanding and change are available to your future mate, too.

We have seen that communication is a vital link between individuals and that developing that ability will help to insure a good marriage and a good relationship with any children you may have.

You were reminded of the responsibility of all human beings toward the claims of the Creator and encouraged to make loyalty to Jesus Christ the first priority in your life.

Next in importance is the selection of your mate, because he should work in partnership with you to make a marriage that will bring out the best qualities in each of you. Ideally, each one will become a more fulfilled person than either of you could be individually and, together, you can make a significant contribution to the stability of good marriages and happy children in our culture. You can become a Christian witness working as a team and reach other couples with the message of God's love.

Once you're engaged, the importance of learning as much as you can about your future mate assumes top priority. Each one has an opportunity to be honest with the other, to accept each other despite your deficiencies, and to help each other in your progress towards improved attitudes and behavior.

Cutting loose implies cutting the umbilical cord of dependency on your parents. We presented the problems involved in making this decision and the price of becoming your own person against parental opposition. In this area we focused on the problem parent, but that doesn't mean that there aren't many mature, understanding parents who relate well to their children and enjoy their relationship.

In the matter of sex, you have seen the influence of

home training on one's attitudes towards this basic human instinct, and the vital necessity of a good marriage relationship in this area.

Goals and commitments to them are the things that cause us to perform. In marriage they provide the basic motivation for the decisions you will make in regard to the use of your time, money, and talents. Goals can tie a marriage together or tear it apart.

And now, with these subjects behind us, let's leave the problems for a time and focus on the positive aspects of the marriage and the first few weeks after the ceremony.

If you and your partner have had counseling sessions before or during the engagement period, then you both have undoubtedly been helping each other to modify your personalities in some respects. This does not mean, however, that you will graduate to perfection as soon as the marriage vows are spoken and the ceremony is over. You will be entering upon a new and more intimate phase of your life during which you both will continue to show some undesirable traits but during which each of you will hopefully continue to help the other.

The difference that the marriage vows will make, however, is real and significant. Before marriage, the emphasis has been on you as an individual—your personal aims, aptitudes, and attitudes. Your mate-to-be also has been engrossed in his own interests. During the courtship time, when you were together, you were beginning to be interested in learning about each other. And you were enjoying being with each other.

During the engagement period this "getting to know you" process was intensified and included finding out each other's attitudes about many deeply held convictions regarding spiritual things, a personal philosophy of living, the attitude towards the roles of the husband and wife, child rearing, one's business or profession, and other areas of living. In recent years I have noticed that a large number of wedding ceremonies include a solemn candle-lighting ritual. All during the ceremony three tapers have been in view behind the altar. The ones on either end are lit, the middle one is not. At one point in the ceremony, frequently right after the clergyman pronounces the couple man and wife and before the final prayer, the couple each take their own lighted candle (hers on her left; his on his right) and together light the taller central candle while each blows out his individual candle. This impressive act symbolizes the unity of the man and his wife. They are now one in God's sight.

Now most of us readily agree to this principle of becoming one, and think immediately of the physical consummation of their marriage as signifying this oneness. It is true, of course, that the intimacy of the marriage union is a primary one, but there is another and important oneness that deserves some consideration here.

The habits of a lifetime are difficult to change and this is never more true than trying to change the *I* concept to the *we* concept. No longer should it be *my house;* it's *ours*. *My* friends and *his* friends become *our* friends. You earn money and your spouse does, too, but it's *our* money. It's a whole new concept and it requires a definite effort to think *we* when you may have been thinking *I* all your life.

There are friends you may have grown up with and with whom many pleasant associations are recalled. The same is probably true of your partner. There are some of these friends, however, whose personalities will appear to be particularly irritating to you or your mate. These friends can continue to be *yours* or *his* but do not feel an obligation to include them in an *our* friends capacity. This can ruin an otherwise enjoyable evening. Instead, plan to enjoy these friends individually. Meet for lunch someday, or dinner when your spouse is at a meeting but with his or her knowledge. It's unwise, though, to encourage the friendship of a former dating partner. Rarely can those who have been involved in a serious relationship break up and still remain comfortable with each other. And if the effort *is* made, there may be feelings of competitiveness displayed between your spouse and your former friend. It is best to sever the relationship completely except for seeing each other during casual encounters at group functions or at the homes of friends with other couples.

The *we* concept is perhaps best illustrated in the spiritual dimension. Although *my* Lord and *your* Lord is also traditionally referred to as *our* Lord in the relationship of brothers in Christ, it has a special emphasis in the case of the husband and wife who are united under the Lordship of Christ. For them, their relationship is a triangular one. God is at the apex and they are at His feet.

When the ceremony has ended and the last piece of cake has been eaten, the bride and groom will leave. Friends will pelt them with rice and wish them well. And these two persons who once were strangers will enter into a relationship that has been ordained by God for the benefit of man. Within the framework of this new family unit will come the children who someday will shape the culture of their time. And hopefully many will hold out the message of love that will shape the destinies of men's souls.

Marriage is both high privilege and solemn responsibility—and a call to an adventure in abundant living under the Lordship of Jesus Christ.

> I am come that they may have life, and that they might have it more abundantly.
>
> John 10:10

QUESTIONS FOR DISCUSSION

1. What vital understanding must a person have about himself and his partner before thinking of entering a marriage relationship?
2. This book has strongly emphasized premarital counseling. What has been it's rationale?
3. How can the Lordship of Christ be practically applied to a marriage relationship?